# THE RISE AND FALL OF THIRD PARTIES

*Is Wallace's third-party movement likely to succeed?*

*What does it have in common with third parties of the past?*

*Why have third parties sprung into being from time to time?*

*Is there a genuine need for a permanent third party at the present time?*

These are some of the key questions which are answered in *The Rise and Fall of Third Parties.*

Vividly written by a keen observer of the political scene, this fascinating book provides a timely analysis of one of the most interesting phenomena of American history. It describes the rise and fall of the Locofocos, the Know-Nothing Party, the Anti-Masonic movement, and other curious growths on the American body politic. It tells the story of some of the major revolts within the Republican and Democratic Parties. And it dissects the Wallace movement in the light of present facts and past tendencies. The obstacles and opportunities of a genuine third party are discussed in the last two chapters.

OTHER BOOKS BY THE AUTHOR

*Twelve Representative Americans*
*Ulysses S. Grant, Politician*
*History of the South*
*South in American History*
*Lincoln and the War Governors*

# THE RISE AND FALL
# OF THIRD PARTIES

*From Anti-Masonry to Wallace*

By WILLIAM B. HESSELTINE

*Professor of History, University of Wisconsin*

## PUBLIC AFFAIRS PRESS
WASHINGTON, D. C.

# INTRODUCTION

Even without Henry Wallace's new movement to bring it into focus, the historical experience of American third parties—not all of them have been "liberal"—is of considerable significance at the present time.

In recent years, many liberals, progressives, farmers and trade unionists have been giving increasing thought to the need for a permanent third party. Long before Wallace launched his candidacy, sundry organizations were considering the possibilities of a new political movement.

The Americans for Democratic Action, an organization composed of ex-New Dealers and miscellaneous liberals, has for sometime been hatching ambitious plans for its special variety of liberalism. Another group, the Committee on Education For a New Party, headed by the Pullman Porters' A. Phillip Randolph, has been studying ways and means of making up a berth in which liberals—strange bed-fellows all—could crowd together. In New York, members of the Liberal Party have been speculating hopefully about expanding on a national scale. In Wisconsin, the Progressives, who suffered ignominious rebuffs when they generously offered to liberalize the Republican Party, have been giving serious consideration to the advisability of revitalizing their movement.

Since none of these groups are at all happy about Henry Wallace's candidacy, it is plainly evident that the dream of and trend toward a genuine third party will continue to be a highly important factor in the American political scene.

5

Certainly this election year is a most propitious time to examine our political present in the light of the history of third parties of the past. True, history cannot provide any sure answers or solutions for our immediate perplexities, but it will contribute substantially to our understanding of how we got this way.

\* \* \*

Although based chiefly upon a series of articles which originally appeared in the weekly *Progressive* and several lectures which were delivered at the University of Maryland under the auspices of the Committee on American Civilization, the contents of this book have been somewhat revised and, in certain respects, expanded.

The author's thanks are due to a host of friends and critics who urged the publication of this book and to others who furnished helpful addenda and corrections. He is especially indebted to Morris Rubin, editor of the *Progressive*, who originally suggested the series which appeared in his publication and whose guidance was invaluable; to George Olson, secretary-treasurer of the Non-Partisan League, for information about his organization; to Alfred C. Lane, McAllister Coleman, and Leon Henderson for advice; to Professor Wesley M. Gewehr of the University of Maryland for critical commentary; and to M. B. Schnapper of Public Affairs Press for skillful editing.

*William B. Hesseltine*
Professor of History
University of Wisconsin

# CONTENTS

# CHAPTER ONE

# THE ROOTS OF REVOLT

Although it would be sheer absurdity to argue that history repeats itself, or that the lessons of history "prove" a third party cannot be successful, it might be well to understand why no "third" party has ever become a major party or achieved success in the nation. All successful new parties have begun as opposition or second parties and have rapidly achieved first place. Thus, Thomas Jefferson organized the anti-Federalists, the Virginia planters, Western frontiersmen, and Aaron Burr's New York artisan followers into the Republicans and won, within four years, the Presidency. Thus, Clay and Webster on the one hand and Jackson on the other reassembled discordant groups into the Whig and Democratic Parties respectively. And the Republicans, too, though a coalescence of dissenters, were never a "third" party, but began as a second party and quickly became the first.

Certainly the evidence of history seems to indicate that a new political movement cannot take time to build slowly and "educate" the voters. A new party must simultaneously educate, recruit members, seek office, and exercise power wherever and whenever possible.

Yet third parties have in the past made distinct contributions to American politics and progressives can learn much from their history. In general, third parties have performed the function of calling attention to serious prob-

lems and pointing a way to their solution. They have stimulated—sometimes by frightening them—the lethargic or
timid politicans of the major parties. They have advocated
reforms which the older parties have adopted and enacted
into law. And sometimes they have trained leaders for
the major parties.

Throughout the nineteenth century a host of third parties appeared and disappeared before the eyes of the American voter. Some of them, like the Workingmen's Party, the
Equal Rights Party, the Anti-Monopolists, the Honest Men's
Party of Massachusetts, or the Readjusters of Virginia were
local in appeal and so transitory that they made no real
impression on the electorate. Others, however, were important movements. Among them were the anti-Masons,
the Liberty and Free Soil Parties, the Know Nothings, the
Liberal Republicans, and the Populists—each of which
threatened the existing parties and forced lasting changes
of policy.

The least important of this group, and the most ephem-
eral in its basic principles, was the Anti-Masonic Party.
Yet in its brief years it foreshadowed some of the major
problems, pitfalls, and performances of future third parties. It began in 1826, when William Morgan, a somewhat down-at-heels citizen of Batavia, N. Y., published a
book which pretended to reveal the secrets of the Masonic
fraternity. Shortly afterwards, Morgan disappeared and
suspicion pointed to the Masons. A popular furor against
the Masons, and other secret societies as well, spread over
Western New York, reached into Pennsylvania, Ohio, New
Jersey, Massachusetts, and Vermont, and became, almost
overnight, a political party.

It was a party which appealed to the poorer classes to

vote against the rich—most of whom, it appeared, were Masons. The party was thus a social upheaval with a strong democratic base. But it was not long before it attracted the attention of ambitious politicians. Thurlow Weed and William H. Seward in New York and Thad Stevens in Pennsylvania saw in anti-Masonry a tool for striking at Jacksonian Democracy. Under their leadership, the party broadened its appeal, coming out for tariffs to protect domestic manufactures, the improvements of canals, and exempting banks from a regulatory tax. The Anti-Masonic Party, appealing to orthodoxy in religion, opposed Unitarianism and other forms of religious liberalism.

In less than a decade the Anti-Masonic Party passed from a movement with a democratic appeal—in which it opposed imprisonment for debt and compulsory militia service—to an organization which formed a popular bulwark for conservatism. In 1832 its Presidential candidate polled seven electoral votes, but by 1836 it was securely captured by the Whig Party.

Yet in its brief existence the Anti-Masons had made two distinct contributions to American society. First, they had called attention to the dangers of secret societies in a democracy and had forced some of them—including Phi Beta Kappa—to come out of hiding. The second contribution of this strange political party was the national nominating convention. In 1832 the Anti-Masons held the first national convention to nominate a Presidential candidate, and the Whigs and the Democrats quickly imitated them. Whatever defects this institution may have developed in its later history, it was more democratic than the nominations-by-caucus system which it displaced.

The course of anti-Masonry from liberalism to reaction

found a parallel in the anti-slavery movement. Opposition to slavery was as old as the institution itself, and in the early days had centered along the democratic Southern frontier. Quakers who practiced democracy and Presbyterians, Methodists, and Baptists who represented the masses damned slavery on moral grounds. In the 1820's a religious revival in the Calvinist sects emphasized the duty of benevolence and stimulated concern over the moral aspects of holding men in bondage.

In 1831 William Lloyd Garrison began publishing the *Liberator* and demanding the immediate abolition of slavery. The next year he founded the New England Anti-Slavery Society, and the following year he helped found the American Anti-Slavery Society. Anti-slavery societies sprang up in all parts of the North and West, and almost immediately they began to participate in politics. They questioned candidates on their attitude towards slavery, and they deluged Congress with petitions to abolish slavery in the District of Columbia. In seven years they were a political party.

William Lloyd Garrison knew that such a moral issue as slavery could not be solved by political devices, and he would have nothing to do with politics. Because the Constitution recognized slavery, he denounced it as a "covenant with Death and an agreement with Hell." With a handful of followers he moved logically to a position where he opposed all human government. With more practicality and less logic other abolitionists determined to vote their principles into law.

In 1840 they formed the Liberty Party and nominated James G. Birney, a Kentuckian who had freed his own slaves, for the Presidency. In 1844 Birney ran again, increasing his vote from 7,100 in 1840 to 62,000 in 1844 and winning enough support in New York to keep the Whig, Henry Clay, from carrying the state. Thereby the Liberty Party succeeded in placing the pro-slavery James K. Polk in the White House.

By virtue of their moral fervor and their humanitarian objective, the Liberty Party should have been liberal. Their basic appeal, however, was to the rising industrial capitalists of the North. Slavery, they argued, threatened the "agricultural, mechanical, manufacturing, and commercial interests of the country." They capitalized upon the depression of 1837, pointing out that Southerners, whose moral depravity was due to slavery, did not pay their debts to Northerners.

Economic recovery after 1844 wrecked the Liberty Party's argument that prosperity and slavery were incompatible. Moreover, the practical men who had hoped to use the party to rise to power grew disappointed over its slow growth. But the Mexican War, which the Liberty men had helped bring about by inadvertently aiding Polk, brought the new problem of the control of the territory which the war added.

Cotton capitalists of the South dreamed of expanding into the area, and of carrying their plantation system into new lands. Northern financial and industrial interests saw the new area as a field for their expansion. The issue was formulated in terms of the expansion of slavery, though it involved much more than the growth of the slave system. In the North, representatives of Northern capital wrapped their lust for Western profits in the words of freedom. Let the West, they said, be given as small farms to "the hardy pioneers of our own land and the oppressed and banished of other lands."

This was a broader base for a party than the Liberty Party had had, and small farmers, villagers, and workers responded. The Van Buren wing—the "Barnburners"—of New York's Democrats split from their party, and "conscience Whigs," opposed to slavery, left the ranks of the Whigs.

In 1844, meeting at Buffalo with Liberty men, these groups formed the Free Soil Party—demanding "Free Soil, Free Speech, Free Labor, and Free Men." They hushed their more extreme abolitionists and nominated Martin Van Buren for President. That year he polled nearly 300,000 votes. Four years later, with an abolitionist, John P. Hale, as the candidate, the Free Soilers got but half as many. The lesson was clear: expediency was more profitable than principle. In 1856 the Free Soil politicians were squabbling with old Whigs and one-time Democrats for places in the new Republican Party.

By the 1850's, when the Free Soil Party was dissolving into the Republican ranks, party lines were breaking down. The Whig Party had won the elections of 1840 and 1848, and both times its President had died and their successors had proven failures.

On the other hand, the Democratic Party, which had, long since abandoned principles of Jefferson and Jackson for conservative "Old Fogeyism," maintained itself—at least in part—by the corrupt use of urban immigrant voters. In the late 1850's Irish immigrants settled in the Eastern cities, while German refugees took up lands in the West. They competed with native Americans in the labor market or took lands which Americans a couple of generations from the immigrant steerage thought that they alone should have.

These new immigrants were clannish, they belonged, many of them, to the Catholic Church, and they voted Democratic. A number of nativist and anti-Catholic societies, expressing alarm over the foreign invasion, gathered members among Protestants and among urban workers. Soon they entered politics, and before the politicians of the older parties knew it, the Native American secret societies won victories at the polls. Soon Whig and Democratic politicians joined the "Know-Nothings" and organized the American Party.

In 1854 the Know-Nothings won complete control of Massachusetts, carried Pennsylvania, and elected a number of Congressmen. The next year, however, the party split on the slavery issue and fell into the hands of Southerners. In 1856 their candidate, Millard Fillmore, polled 875,000 popular votes and won Maryland's eight electoral votes. But by that time Northern Know-Nothings had joined the more promising Republican Party.

After the party realignments in the middle of the 1850's no significant third parties appeared until Grant's administration. During the Civil War, the politicians cried loudly for political unity, even while factionalism rent the ranks of the Republican Party. From that factional strife the interests of big business, of bankers and bondholders, of railroad land-grabbers and of protected manufacturers came eventually to dominate the party. The politicians of the party grew steadily more corrupt, while the party rested largely upon the corrupt, Army-dominated Negro vote of the South.

Liberals in the party—some of them old abolitionists, some Western agrarians, and some tariff reformers—began to attack this system of "Grantism." They correctly identified the source of the evils in the vindictive reconstruction of the South.    In 1870 Missouri's liberals broke away from the Republicans, formed the "Liberal Republican Party," and won their state.    In 1872, civil service reformers, free traders, and friends of states rights launched the Liberal Republican Party on a national scale—and promptly sore-headed politicians who had been deprived of the patronage by other corruptionists, joined them, took control of the Cincinnati convention out of the hands of well-meaning but inept reformers, and wangled the party's nomination for Horace Greeley, a high tariff spoilsman as bad as any of Grant's predatory henchmen.    The Democrats, inspired by a desire to take "anything to beat Grant" also nominated Greeley—and thereby completed the perversion of liberalism.

Though the Liberal Republican movement proved abortive, conditions under Republican rule in the age of big business produced a succession of third party movements. Out of the exploited West came the Granger movement which endorsed candidates and the Greenback Party which ran Presidential candidates in 1876 and 1880.    In 1878 the Greenbackers polled a million votes and elected 15 Congressmen on a program of inflating the currency.    Finally, continued exploitation by banks, machinery companies, trusts and railroads produced the Populist movement, the greatest third party of the 19th Century.

The Peoples Party began in the grain growing states and spread into the South.    Agricultural Wheels and Farmers Alliances joined forces with money reformers who wanted greenbacks and free silver and with Knights of Labor who favored One Big Union to launch a national party.    Their platform in 1892 began with one of the most vigorous political philippics in Anglo-American literature:

"We meet in the midst of a nation brought to the verge of moral, political, and material ruin.  Corruption dominates the ballot box, the Legislatures, the Congress, and touches even the ermine of the bench.  The people are demoralized. . . . The newspapers are largely subsidized or muzzled, public opinion silenced, business prostrated, homes covered with mortgages, and the land concentrating into the hands of capitalists.  The urban workmen are denied the right to organize for self protection . . . and they are rapidly degenerating into European conditions. The fruits of the toil of millions are boldly stolen to build up colossal fortunes for the few. . . . From the same prolific womb of governmental injustice we breed the two great classes—tramps and millionaires."

With this preamble, the Peoples Party advocated Government ownership of railroads, telephones and telegraph, abolition of national banks, free coinage of silver, a graduated income tax, postal savings banks, the end of Government land grants to railroads, one term for the President, the initiative and referendum, and restriction of immigration—the whole gamut of liberal and reform ideas.

For a moment it appeared the Populists would achieve major party status.  In 1892 they won 22 electoral votes, sent a dozen avowed Populists and a number of sympathisers to Congress, elected three governors and hundreds of state legislators.  But after this promising beginning the Populists went the way of all third parties.  They began to think that they could capture one of the old parties, and in 1896 they rallied behind Bryan.  In making the fusion, they abandoned a good half of their principles and staked their all on the issue of the free coinage of silver.

By 1900 the effort of a handful of devotees to revive the party was completely futile.

Yet the Populist cause was not entirely lost with the Peoples Party. The income tax, postal savings banks, banking reform, and other items in the Populist agenda became law in the years to come, while Populist ideas permeated both the Democratic and Republican Parties.

This, after all, was the historic function of third party movements. In the nineteenth century the Liberal Republicans, the Free Soilers, the Anti-Masons, and even the Know-Nothings had called attention to social and political evils and had marshalled support of reforms. A large portion of their proposals had found place on the statute books. Without the third parties reaction, "Old Fogeyism," "Grantism," and monopoly would have reigned unchecked.

If those who are in favor of a new party are content to remain missionaries, they might find much comfort in the record of achievement of the nineteenth century's third parties.

# CHAPTER TWO

# THE BULL MOOSE MOVEMENT

The twentieth century, now nearly half gone, has seen many of the aspirations of the nineteenth century's third parties fulfilled. The Populist cause did not die with the People's Party, but lived on to invigorate both the Democrats and the Republicans. Bryanism among the Democrats and insurgency among the Republicans were alike remnants of nineteenth century Populism. Within twenty years after 1892's high tide of Populism, the "Bull Moose" Progressives came closer to success than any third party in American history.

The story of the Progressive Party of 1912 is a sordid lesson of how a liberal cause can be betrayed. Idealists who dream of a new party might well draw caution's counsel from the frustration which expediency brought upon the Bull Moose.

The roots of the Progressives of 1912 were grounded in the soil where Populism and the Knights of Labor had flourished. After the collapse of the People's Party the agrarian ideals of the Populists and the liberal labor principles of the Knights found other—and sounder—expression. Populism had been founded upon emotion and had been preached like a revival. Its rallies were political camp-meetings, and its leaders were evangelists. Its ideas entered into the souls of men, and they emerged in another expression.

The new expression was literary. By the beginning of

the twentieth century a group of journalists had begun to explore the mechanics of big business, and a number of new and vigorous magazines had sprung into existence to carry their stories to a public that moved from incredulity to indignation. Within a few years such magazines as the *American, McClure's, Collier's* and *Everybody's* had carried Ida Tarbell's "History of the Standard Oil Company," Thomas W. Lawson's "Frenzied Finance" exposing Amalgamated Copper, and Ray S. Baker's "The Railroads on Trial."

In 1905, Upton Sinclair's *The Jungle* disclosed conditions in the Chicago meat-packing industry, and in 1905-06 David G. Phillip's "Treason of the Senate," running in *The Cosmopolitan,* showed that 75 of the 90 U. S. Senators were hirelings of railroads, the beef and sugar trusts, and Standard Oil. Lincoln Steffens published "The Shame of the Cities" and "Enemies of the Republic," dealing with municipal and state corruption, in *McClure's,* and Samuel Adams exposed patent medicines in the pages of *Collier's.* The "Muckrakers"—as Theodore Roosevelt called them in disgust—exposed the banks and insurance companies, revealed the evils of child labor, and pried into commercial vice.

The muckrakers succeeding in alarming the middle classes who had been relatively unmoved by evangelical Populism. As a result of muckraking exposures a wave of reform began in cities and states. "Golden Rule" Jones and Brand Whitlock in Toledo and Tom Johnson in Cleveland were reform mayors under whose leadership the people turned against their oppressors and began municipal ownership of public utilities.

In St. Louis J. W. Folk and in Denver Judge Ben Lindsey fought the political machines. In Minneapolis a Grand Jury under H. C. Clark uncovered the Ames Ring, and in 1910 Emil Seidel became mayor of Milwaukee and began an era of good government which lasted three decades. In addition, the cities experimented with new forms of government: Galveston began the commission form, and Staunton, Va., pioneered the city manager plan. Municipal home rule permitted the cities to write their own charters to deal with their own problems.

Most of these municipal reforms were in the Populist areas of the Middle West, and there the movement spread from the municipal to the state governments. "Fighting Bob" LaFollette became governor of Wisconsin, J. W. Folk became governor of Missouri, A. B. Cummings won Iowa, and Hiram Johnson was elected in California. Even in New York the reformers elected Charles E. Hughes. In their states these men fought the political machines. They broke down the boss-dominated convention system, and in 1903 Wisconsin adopted the first state primary law. In other states the initiative and referendum and the recall were enacted into law. The reformers secured social legis-- lation—limiting the hours of women in industry, restricting child labor, imposing the eight-hour day on public works, and making employers assume responsibility for health conditions in factories.

This was the progressive movement—intelligent planned reforms which restored government to the people. In many respects the movement came to its finest flower in Wisconsin, where a happy combination of the state university and skillful political leadership set an example to the nation. Guided by a liberal-minded president, the University of Wisconsin had added to the faculty a number of young scholars who, because they pried too inquisitively into the mechanics of society, were unwelcome in other institutions. Many of them had been trained in the seminars of Johns Hopkins University and had learned new methods of research in the social sciences. Their techniques of investigation were better, and their conclusions sounder, than those of the muckraking journalists. Though their literary style was poorer, their indignation over conditions they discovered was as intense as that of the muckrakers. These social scientists—Richard Ely, John R. Commons, Edward Alsworth Ross, and Frederick Jackson Turner, to mention but a few—worked in the great liberal university at Madison in a political climate prepared by Populism.

The lessons they taught were given application by "Fighting Bob" LaFollette. Almost literally, LaFollette sat in the seminars of these masters of the new learning, taking their abstract findings and translating them into the language of the political stump. He won the governorship of Wisconsin, and promptly began to put the new ideas into practice. The university professors joined the governor, trained men for the offices of the government, advised ,and studied. Governors and professors together made doctoral dissertations into political institutions. Dr. Charles McCarthy developed the Legislative Reference Library. Prof. John R. Commons drafted labor legislation. And the unofficial "extension-lecturer" LaFollette educated the electorate and organized them into a solid political group. Wisconsin became a laboratory of democratic political experiments, and the world watched its progress.

Although Bryanites among the Democrats sometimes helped, these progressive groups in the Middle West worked within the Republican Party for the most part. In large measure, they were held in the party of Big Business by the political acumen of two men: Mark Hanna and Theodore Roosevelt. Hanna—who has long since become identified in the popular mind as a plutocrat—was himself a Middle Western industrialist who understood some of the Western problems. Moreover, he had a sincere interest in the well-being of the laboring men. Thanks to Hanna's intelligent leadership, the Republicans tried to give the workers a "full dinner pail," and the laboring men stayed in the Republican ranks.

Theodore Roosevelt, on the other hand, had neither sympathy with nor understanding of the progressive movement. He was a militarist and an imperialist. He had reformed New York's inefficient and corrupt police, but he was no reformer. He had brought order into the Navy Department and made the Navy ready for the war with Spain. He believed in using the "Big Stick" freely.

In his younger days he had written history, but he did so without gaining the human sympathy of a Frederick Jackson Turner, nor the economic insight of a Charles Beard. Tom Paine, the revolutionist, was only "a dirty little atheist" to Theodore Roosevelt. At the same time that Turner was assessing the "significance of the frontier" in spreading democracy over the land, Roosevelt, too, was writing about the "Winning of the West." But the Harvard man saw the Western movement only as a military conquest. Roosevelt believed that a twelve-hour day for street-car motormen was un-American socialism. He favored contract prison labor, opposed pensions for teachers, and commended President Cleveland for sending troops to suppress the Pullman strikers.

But Theodore Roosevelt was also a politician, ambitious for office, and eager to preserve the Republican Party. He recognized the need for reform without accepting the progressive dogma that reforms must be democratic. As President, Roosevelt adopted enough of the progressive program to keep the Middle Western progressives from bolting the Republican Party—the Pure Food and Drugs Act, an employers' liability law, conservation, and the Hepburn Act regulating railroad rates.

With an eye upon the headlines, he breathed fire against the trusts—though he seldom followed through a prosecution. In general, he extended the area of government control—as a true militarist would do—without extending the area of democracy. The total effect of this regime was the strengthening of monopolistic interests. Reformers of the LaFollette type believed Roosevelt a compromiser and an insincere politician. Such old Populists as South Carolina's Ben Tillman found him temporizing and timid.

The progressive forces which had acquiesced in Roosevelt's reforms broke out in insurgency under William Howard Taft. With Roosevelt in Africa hunting big game, the big business interests which he had not stalked came to the fore. Promptly they attempted to raise tariff rates, and Middle Western progressives joined the Democrats to oppose the bill. In the Senate, Bob LaFollette, Albert J. Beveridge, A. J. Cummins, Knute Nelson and other progressives fought the Payne-Aldrich measure item by item at every opportunity.

At almost the same time, Victor Murdock and George W. Norris in the House of Representatives led a fight against the powerful position of the reactionary speaker,

"Uncle Joe" Cannon. These legislative fights divided the GOP, and a struggle between Secretary of the Interior Ballinger and Chief Forester Gifford Pinchot over alleged attempts of the former to give mineral and waterpower sites to big corporations drove the progressives from the Republicans. In 1910, Democrats won control of Congress.

Early in 1911 the progressives formed the Progressive Republican League and began to lay plans to win control of the party. They advocated progressive social and economic legislation, and proposed as well the direct election of Senators, direct primaries for nominations, direct election of delegates to national conventions, and the initiative and referendum. On this program they began to line up for Bob LaFollette.

As progressivism and insurgency became militant, Roosevelt and the conservatives took alarm. George W. Perkins of U. S. Steel and International Harvester and Publisher Frank Munsey began to urge Roosevelt to come forward. Munsey advised Roosevelt that "my observation and reasoning as I study these problems at home and abroad leads unerringly to the conclusion that the state has got to swing back a bit from our vaunted Republicanism and take on a more parental guardianship of the people."

"The people," continued Munsey, "need safeguarding in their investments, their savings, their application of conservation. They need encouragement, the sustaining and guiding hand of the state. They need the German system of helping them to save money for their old age."

"It is the work of the state," explained the publisher, "to think for the people and plan for the people—to teach them how to do, what to do, and to sustain them in the doing."

With this advice before him, Roosevelt needed little more urging. Personally piqued at Taft, whom he blamed for having widened the party breach, the ex-President announced his candidacy in February, 1912, and proclaimed his endorsement of the Progressives' principles.

Promptly the alarmed reactionaries began a smear campagn to head off LaFollette. They insisted that the Wisconsin statesman was too intellectual—what the party needed was Roosevelt's emotional appeal. They insinuated that LaFollette was too radical; that he was, in fact, a socialist—while the party needed a man who was only a little left of center. When finally LaFollette showed fatigue from his long campaign, Roosevelt of the strenuous life and the men of U. S. Steel launched a vicious whispering campaign that Fighting Bob's mind was gone.

The smear campaign had its effect. Throughout the progressive region the states sent delegates to the Republican convention instructed for Roosevelt. When the Taft men, controlling the convention, rejected progressive delegations, the insurgents refused to co-operate. As the boss-ridden convention nominated Taft, the more insidously boss-ridden progressives demanded that Roosevelt lead them to victory.

They formed a new party, and Roosevelt arrived, feeling "fit as a Bull Moose" to lead them. They adopted a platform with all the Populist-Progressive planks—direct primaries, direct election of Senators, woman suffrage, corrupt practices acts, conservation, a department of labor, the eight-hour day—and the usual denunciation of the "unholy allegiance between corrupt business and corrupt politics."

Led by the popular and dramatic Teddy, the Progressives campaigned vigorously and brought defeat to Taft's old guard. In the electoral college Taft got but eight votes while Roosevelt polled 88—and Woodrow Wilson, with a minority of the popular vote, got 435 electoral votes.

The final act in the betrayal of the progressive cause came four years later. The Wilson Administration enacted a large body of progressive legislation, and many Progressives joined the Democrats. Out of office, the old guard Republicans grew even more reactionary. By the election of 1916, the time was ripe for the Progressives to reap the harvest they had sowed in 1912. Then, with one stroke, they had become a second party and relegated the Taft faction to a poor third party status. But Roosevelt and the magnates of International Harvester and U. S. Steel were not interested in perpetuating the Progressive Party. They were more concerned with resuscitating the Republicans. Roosevelt advised the Progressives to return to their political home. When the discouraged Progressives met in convention, Roosevelt refused to lead them again. He announced his own support of Charles Evans Hughes. Leaderless and divided, the Progressives drifted to the Democrats and re-elected Wilson.

Thus the greatest "third" party in American history passed ignominiously from the scene, deluded into expediency and betrayed by its pseudo-progressive leader.

# CHAPTER THREE

# THE PROGRESSIVES OF 1924

If the Bull Moose experience demonstrated that principles should not be sacrificed to expediency, the chief lesson of the Progressive third party of 1924 is that a third-party movement needs a well-grounded local organization to be a success.

The Progressive Party of 1924 learned that elections cannot be won by a devoted leader, high-minded principles, and burning issues. A successful party must have leg-work as well as brain work, door-bell pushers as well as spellbinders, and an army of aspirants for local offices whose jobs depend on their getting out the vote.

The Bull Moose Party of 1912 had such an army of precinct workers, and in its first campaign it won second place in the Electoral College. But the Bull Moose Party was a split from a major party, and the division went all the way down to the wards. The Roosevelt Progressives had a full-bodied party with local units of fighting strength.

The Progressives of 1924, however, were a true "third" party, and their local organizations were, for the most part, feeble or non-existent. In 1912 Roosevelt could talk—in the militarist idiom he loved—about how "we stand at Armageddon and battle for the Lord," and he spoke for a host of captains, lieutenants, and privates in the ranks. In 1924 Bob LaFollette's followers had no more fighting strength than had the dozen shivering Jews who huddled at the gates of Gethsemane.

This was tragic, for in the middle of the 20's the United States badly needed a well-organized progressive movement. The Democrats and the Republicans vied with each other for conservatism: the Democrats had descended from Wilson, through Cox, to wind up with John W. Davis. The Republicans, rescued from Harding by the grim reaper, were keeping cool with Coolidge. The time was clearly ripe for a revival of the Progressive Party.

The utter mediocrity of the Republican and Democratic leaders only served to emphasize the spiritual degradation of the country. For four years after 1912, the Wilson Administration had stolen planks from the Bull Moose platform and built them into laws. But after 1916 and the collapse of the Progressive Party the Wilson Administration moved rapidly into a war that was to make the world unsafe for both democracy and progressivism. At the close of the war, the Democrats put on a "red hunt," burned socialistic witches, and gave shelter to the Ku Klux Klan. The Republicans, gaining power in 1920, rapidly came under the sway of the "Ohio gang" and staged a series of scandals ranging from those at the Veterans Bureau to Teapot Dome.

Meantime, under the beneficent "return to normalcy," the Shipping Board had sold to private operators the war-built merchant fleet at a fraction of its value; Congress reduced taxes on big corporations and passed the Fordney-McCumber tariff raising rates to the highest point in American history; the Federal Trade Commission smiled at the growth of monopolies, and the Supreme Court blocked social legislation.

But in these years, despite the spiritual decline and the dominance of reaction, progressivism was not dead. Bob

LaFollette and the Progressive Republicans co-operated in putting through reform legislation in Wilson's first Administration. Many of them clung to their principles when Wilson abandoned reform for militarism. LaFollette opposed American intervention in the First World War, and throughout the Middle Western home of progressivism liberals divided on the war. Enough of them, however, opposed the imperialist venture, the vengeful Treaty of Versailles, and the war-stimulated growth of monopoly to keep the progressive movement alive.

When economic collapse followed the war and a depressed agriculture failed to recover, the progressive movement began again to take political form. Through the war the Nonpartisan League had kept agrarian radicalism alive and had spread over the wheatlands. In 1920 a Farmer-Labor Party, centering in Minnesota, ran P. P. Christensen for President, and in 1922-23 it sent Henrik Shipstead and Magnus Johnson to the Senate. In that body, under LaFollette's leadership, Shipstead and Johnson joined North Dakota's Lynn Frazier, Smith Brookhart of Iowa, and Democrat Burton K. Wheeler of Montana in a Farm Bloc which frustrated Secretary of the Treasury Mellon's tax program and carried on a steady fight for agriculture. Nominally most of these men were Republicans, but they and their allies in the House of Representatives held the balance of power in the Congress elected in 1922. Their position as Republicans was uncomfortable if not untenable, and they began to long for a truly liberal party.

In February, 1922, at LaFollette's house in Washington, a gathering of liberals, in and out of Congress, organized the Conference for Progressive Political Action. To its support came the railroad brotherhoods, and a group of liberal intellectuals led by *The Nation* and *The New Republic*. The American Federation of Labor smiled encouragement, and the Socialist Party gave hints of support. The CPPA participated in the Congressional elections of 1922, and their success inspired them to form a separate party for the Presidential election of 1924.

On July 4, 1924, a convention of the Conference for Progressive Political Action at Cleveland launched the new Progressive Party and offered its nomination to "Fighting Bob" LaFollette. The Senator, just past his 69th birthday and in failing health, valiantly accepted this last chance to battle for progressive principles. He helped choose Burton K. Wheeler for his running mate, and he wrote the platform of the new party.

"The great issue before the American people today is the control of government and industry by private monopoly," the platform began .

"For a generation the people have struggled patiently, in the face of repeated betrayals by successive administrations, to free themselves from this intolerable power which has been undermining representative government."

Then LaFollette launched into a many-sided attack upon the institutions of monopoly—the executive departments, the courts, and the militarist system. Specifically, he proposed to recover naval oil reserves, revise the water power act and develop Muscle Shoals, reduce taxes and collect war loans from foreign governments, reconstruct the Federal Reserve System, and reform the Interstate Commerce Commission. He favored public ownership of water power and railroads, and strict control over the developments of the nation's coal, oil, and mineral resources. He proposed

ending the injunction in labor disputes, and he denounced
the doctrine of judicial review. He proposed to elect Federal judges for 10 year terms.

Finally, LaFollette condemned a foreign policy manip-
ulated in the interests of "financial imperialists, oil monopolies, and international bankers" and proposed revising the
war-breeding Versailles Treaty and the negotiation of trea-
ties to "outlaw wars, abolish conscription, drastically reduce land, air, and naval armaments, and guarantee public
referendum on peace and war."

The platform and the candidate represented the finest
flower of the American liberal tradition. The American
Federation of Labor, for the first time in its history, endorsed the Progressive Party, and the Socialist Party, for
the only time in its history, abandoned its own organization to accept LaFollette.

LaFollette's candidacy promptly attracted the fire of
both the Republicans and the Democrats. Neither the personalities of Calvin Coolidge and John W. Davis, nor the
programs they endorsed, attracted popular interest. The
orators of both old parties, finding their own candidates so
much alike, turned their execrations upon the Middle Western radical. In particular they pounced upon LaFollette's
attack upon the courts, the ancient Palladium of Liberty—
for the monopolies.

The Progressive campaign concentrated upon obtaining
success for the national ticket to the exclusion of state and
local contests. LaFollette supporters for local officers
were encouraged to seek places on the Democratic or Republican tickets. In some states the Progressives could not
get on the ballot. In others, LaFollette ran as a Socialist.
Only in Wisconsin, Minnesota, and North Dakota were

there substantial state organizations to help him.

The election showed some curious phenomena. Only 51.1% of the voters went to the polls. Of those who went, 15,725,000 voted for Coolidge, 8,386,500 for Davis, and 4,822,900 for LaFollette. The electoral vote was Coolidge 382, Davis 136, and LaFollette 13. The Progressives had carried only Wisconsin. But in 11 other states—all of them west of the Mississippi—the Progressives relegated the Democrats to third place.

The lesson that a party needed local candidates, ward-heelers, and door-bell ringers was made more obvious by the Congressional returns. The 69th Congress, elected in 1924, had a majority of stalwart Coolidge Republicans, and the Party's insurgents no longer held a balance of power. Seven months after the election LaFollette died. In 1928 the forces which had followed Old Bob in his last crusade gave spiritless support to the relatively liberal Al Smith in his campaign against Herbert Hoover. The New Economic Era which followed led into the Great Depression—all of which might have been avoided had the Progressives of 1924 been successful.

# CHAPTER FOUR

# THE SOCIALISTS

In the course of the past fifty years, while progressivism has waxed and waned and a Progressive Party has twice risen and collapsed, the Socialist Party has stood holding a dim red light and beckoning to the shy voters who avert their eyes and hurry past. Each time liberals have sighed for a third party, the Socialists have hastened to point out that the United States has had a third party for years and years. Only the Prohibition Party has had a longer existence as a "third" party—and Socialists cannot understand why the mass of liberals ignore them and why the voters shy away.

The question why liberals and voters reject the Socialists has had many—and generally unconvincing—answers. The two most commonly given—that socialism is an alien philosophy and that its name repels support—seem to fervent Socialists both specious and absurd. Repeatedly some hopeful member—usually a newcomer in the Socialist ranks—arrives at the conclusion that the party should change its name to dodge the smears of its opponents. Promptly some old-timer reminds him that a rose by any other name would have the same odor, that the Methodists and the Quakers have proudly adopted and worn labels that began as epithets. For 46 years the Socialists have clung to their name, while splinters from the party have failed even more dismally in attracting purchasers for their goods under new brand names.

No more valid is the criticism that socialism is an alien philosophy. Despite the vague verbal adherence that Socialists give to the gospel according to St. Karl, the American Socialists are about as close to Karl Marx as American Methodists are to John Wesley. And aside from some antiquated cliches about the workers of the world, and a somewhat more-than-average awareness of foreign affairs, the Socialist Party is about as international as the International Federation of Steamfitters and less so than the Presbyterian Church.

Historically, the Socialist Party of the United States dates from the last decades of the nineteenth century. In 1864 Karl Marx organized his First International and received some sympathetic support from the American labor movement. In 1869 the National Labor Union, which was trying vainly to enter politics as a third party, sent a delegate to the First International. This movement collapsed, and in 1872 the "international" office of the First International was moved to New York in the futile hope of reviving world-wide socialism.

In 1876, the Socialist Labor Party, an independent group with no affiliation with the decadent Marxists, held a national convention and committed itself to a program of winning labor support. Though a handful of sectarian idealists remained faithful and kept the "party" alive, the movement got no place until Edward Bellamy's *Looking Backward,* published in 1887, stimulated interest in a socialist America. The book sold half a million copies, and the author founded a Nationalist movement to promote its sale and advance its principles.

Among the converts to the Nationalist movement was Daniel De Leon, a former West Indian who had been for a time, lecturer in Latin American diplomacy at Columbia University. In 1883, De Leon had supported Henry George's campaign for mayor of New York, and in 1884 he had joined the Knights of Labor. But neither Bellamy's political book-club nor the Knights could absorb De Leon's aggressive energies. In 1890 he joined the Socialist Labor Party and quickly became its national lecturer and the editor of its house organ.

De Leon's personality and his ideas became firmly grafted on the Socialist Labor Party. Aggressive and domineering in the party, he was privately genial and friendly. He was single-minded in his devotion to the workers, and a doctrinaire fanatic in advocating their cause. He denounced both the Knights of Labor and the American Federation of Labor and demanded an industrial organization of the workers which would seize and operate the tools of production. In 1895 he led a secession from the Knights and formed the Socialist Trade and Labor Alliance. A decade later De Leon led this group into the Industrial Workers of the World. But his affiliation with the IWW lasted only three years. In 1908 he led another secession which formed the Workers International Industrial Union.

De Leon's tactics bred factionalism. In 1899 a group within the Socialist Labor Party, losing a fight to oust De Leon, seceded from the party. Under the leadership of Victor Berger and Eugene V. Debs, they formed the Social Democratic Party which, in 1901, changed its name to the Socialist Party of America. Thereafter, though its verbal militancy became fiercer than ever, De Leon's Socialist Labor Party declined rapidly while, for a dozen years, the Socialist Party grew rapidly.

By 1912 the Socialist Party had reached the peak of its

appeal to the electorate. In 1900, with Debs as its Presidential candidate, it polled nearly 97,000 votes. In 1904, Debs received 402,000, in 1908 he got 420,000 and in 1912 nearly 900,000. In 1910 the Socialists elected Emil Seidel mayor of Milwaukee and sent Victor Berger to the House of Representatives in Washington. In 1912 more than 300 state and municipal officials were elected on Socialist tickets.

This growth was accompanied by a sloughing-off of Marxist idioms and the adoption of the vocabulary and the ideas of traditional American radicalism. In 1908 the party had forgotten about "bourgeois" and "proletarians" and could write its platform in English: "The struggle between wage-earners and capitalists grows ever fiercer and has now become the only vital issue before the American people." In 1912 the Socialists could point an accusing finger at the "Capitalist system that is responsible for the increasing burden of armaments, the poverty slums, child labor, most of the insanity, crime and prostitution, and much of the disease that afflicts mankind."

These were words that sprang from Populism rather than from Marxism. So, too, was the program the Socialists endorsed. Like the Populists before them, Socialists demanded "collective ownership and democratic management" of railroads and the telegraph and telephone system. They wanted municipal ownership of grain elevators and stockyards. They proposed to reclaim the swamps, reforest the timberlands, and rebuild the soil. Unlike the Populists, who would abolish the national banks, the Socialists wanted the banking system collectively owned and democratically managed.

Thus by 1912 the Socialists had forgotten whatever foreign origin they might have had and become, in effect, another variant on the old Populist stem. They had, in fact, moved away from Marx and had almost reached Henry George. Their 1912 platform demanded the collective ownership of land, "and in cases where such ownership is impracticable, the appropriation by taxation of the annual rental of all land held for speculation or exploitation."

But not even this evolution into neo-Populism could pull the Socialists higher at the polls. Their history after 1912 is a long record of internal division, factionalism, and decline. In 1916 Debs declined to run again, and Allen Benson gleaned but 585,000 votes in a campaign where all liberals were voting for the man who "kept us out of war." The next year, just as Wilson led the country into war, the party's convention, meeting in St. Louis, denounced the war and advised party members to resist it by all means in their power. Promptly a body of dissenters who believed the Kaiser was planning to conquer the world and who thought that war—being a democratic process—would make the world safe for democracy, withdrew from the party. Debs, however, remained loyal to his principles, resisted the war, and landed in a Federal penitentiary. In 1920, still behind bars, he was again the party's nominee and polled 919,799 votes.

This was a higher total than Debs' vote in 1912 but in the interval woman suffrage had substantially doubled the electorate. In 1912 Debs had won 6% of the voters: in 1920 the Socialist vote was half as much. Thereafter, the Socialist vote declined both absolutely and relatively. In 1924 the Socialists endorsed Bob LaFollette for President, but in 1928, under Norman Thomas, they re-entered the contest. That year Thomas received 267,000 votes. In

1932, with depression in the land, his vote was 882,000. Four years later, with Alf Landon challenging the New Deal and William Lemke challenging everyone, Thomas won 188,000 in a total popular vote of more than 45 million. In 1940 the Socialist vote fell to 99,000 while the total votes cast rose to nearly 50 million. In 1944, Thomas' total dipped still lower—to 80,000—in a total vote of 48,000,000.

These years of decline were characterized by successsive factional splits from the Socialist Party. The "patriots" who deserted the "pacifist" party on the war issue in 1917 never returned. In 1919 the Communist wing, which wanted to affiliate with Moscow and take orders from the Comintern, seceded from the more conservative group and promptly proceeded to split into a multitude of sects.

By 1924 there were 16 "Communist" political parties, differing among themselves over doctrine and device, but each proclaiming itself the true heir of Lenin. With these factions went most of the energy and zeal of the Socialist movement. The Milwaukee *Leader* and the daily New York *Call* passed out of existence and the weekly *Appeal to Reason* disappeared from the newsstands. The soap-boxes with their earnest youths disappeared, as well, from the streets corners. Only in Milwaukee, where a "gutter socialism" had come to represent mostly "good government" did the Socialists hold out, but even there the party eventually lost power and its leaders took jobs in the Roosevelt bureaucracy.

The remaining right-wing, anti-communist Socialist Party faced further division as the New Deal Administration moved into a war program. Steadily the Socialists lost members to the New Deal and to New York's American

Labor Party.  Eventually the party faced the same problem that had confronted it in 1917.  By 1937 the pro-Roosevelt, pro-war factions withdrew to form the Social Democratic Federation—taking with it more of the party's talent.

In reality, both the factionalism and the declining strength of the Socialist Party were symptomatic of a deeper malady. The Socialists were never able, despite the vigor of their words, to bring together agrarian radicals of the West and the liberal-labor forces of the industrial centers.  Consistently, the words of the party were the words of industrial labor, but the party's potential strength lay among the descendants of Populism.  In 1912 the dues-paying members of the party numbered 117,984 and the highest number, in proportion to population, were found in the Western states.  Nevada, Washington, Idaho, Wyoming, Montana, Arizona, Oregon, Oklahoma, North Dakota, Minnesota, California, and Colorado—in that order—had the highest proportion of members.  Wisconsin stood 13th on the list. Rural Utah had relatively more Socialists than industrial Pennsylvania; Kansas more than Ohio; Texas and Florida more than New York.  In Oklahoma there were five non-socialists to each Socialist: In New York the figures were 22 to 1.  Yet despite this clear indication of agrarian strength, the party's platform concentrated on industrial reform with only the most casual reference to agricultural problems.

On the other hand, the Socialist Party has shown no knack for appealing to organized labor.  De Leon denounced the "labor fakers" who led labor when the Knights of Labor were in flower.  Debs fought against the American Federation of Labor, promoting first the rival American Railroad Union and then the IWW.  The party favored industrial unionism, rather than craft unions, but by the time the CIO began as an adventure in industrial unionism in the 1930's, the new organization was oriented toward the Democrats and open to Communist infiltration.

In the light of the confused philosophy, the declining popular support, and the fractioning factionalism of the Socialists, perhaps the real question is "why does the party survive?" The answer is to be found in the personal integrity and moral character of its leaders. Gene Debs and Norman Thomas, both of them more preachers than policians, succeeded in surrounding themselves with faithful, sincere idealists.

The Socialist appeal has always been more moral than political, more concerned with educating in principles than in bargaining for votes, more intellectual than "realistic." Only once—when they supported the Progressives in 1924 —have the Socialists abandoned their organization. At other times the "practical" elements have deserted to Communism, to the New Deal, or to reformism.

In fact, the Socialists substitute a Christian for a Marxian dialectic. The Marxists hold the dictatorship of the proletariat to be inevitable in the evolution of history. The Socialists accept the Christian dialectic that righteousness will eventually prevail by the power of its examples. Awaiting the millenium, the Socialist Party remains righteous.

Long ago, Gene Debs faced the issue whether the party should "soil itself with the dirt of practical politics and the bargain counter?" His answer was clear: "We can have a vote-getting machine and go to perdition with it; or we can have the Cooperative Commonwealth and working-class government. *But we cannot have both.*"

# CHAPTER FIVE

# LABOR SATELLITE PARTIES

Progressives and liberals who have advocated the establishment of a new political party have long deluded themselves with the belief that farmers and laborers, since they are alike exploited by the managers of industrial capital, can be easily brought together in a democratic, progressive, and permanent political organization. Political analysts, agreeing with the liberals, point out that farmers and industrial workers together constitute a majority of the population—and if they would only get together, they could dominate the nation.

For the most part, experience indicates that this thesis is dubious. In simple fact, farmers and workers do not generally work together, and their failure to cooperate should not be an excuse for recrimination or excoriation. Instead, it should lead to a reexamination of the theory that farmers and workers have common interests and a common objective.

An economic analysis of the basic theory of farmer-labor unity might well reveal that neither farmers nor laborers constitute a single coherent group. The interests of workers in heavy industry, railroad laborers, and employees in service industries may be only superficially alike, while the concerns of cotton growers, dairy farmers, wheat raisers, and orchardists may be in fundamental conflict with one another.

Whatever the conclusions of economic investigation may be, it is clear that historically the basic conflicts in American experience have been between industry and agriculture. During the first half century of independence, the interests of agriculture dominated the nation. Western migration, the expansion of the national domain in the interests of agriculture, the War of 1812, the Mexican War, the Seminole War, and the Black Hawk War were major events of the period, while land speculation was a primary economic activity and land laws were the landmarks of legislation.

But in those years industry rose and industrial interests gained strength to challenge the agricultural domination. The Civil War marked the victory of industry, and since Lee's surrender the nation's major problems—tariff, monopolies, concentrated credit, labor disputes, the unequal distribution of wealth, and imperialism—have grown out of industrial supremacy. Agriculture has fought a losing fight, and depression has regularly stalked the farmlands. The historic foe of the farmer has been industry —and mill hands and the captains of industry are alike the exploiters of the man with the hoe.

But American industry cannot be resolved, unfortunately, into such simple terms as agriculture versus industry. Within both agriculture and industry there has been a conflict between the haves and the have-nots, the owners and the owned, the Bigs and the Littles. Not only has the American scene been divided horizontally between industry and agriculture, it has also been divided, in each segment, between a right and a left.

There are in American history (Marxists please note) four great and basic traditions. Two of them are right-wing, representing the interests of property. One is the

Hamiltonian tradition of industrial, commercial, and financial capital. Out of that tradition have come the protective tariff and the national banks, the Liberty League and the NAM. The other is the Bourbon tradition in agriculture, represented in political history by John C. Calhoun, the planter aristocrats, the squires of the Hudson Valley, the Southern Confederacy, the Cattlemen's associations, and the King Ranch.

In conflict with each of these right-wing traditions have been two traditions on the left. One, in constant antagonism to the Hamiltonian tradition, has been the liberal-labor tradition of the urban and industrial centers. The Lib-Labs have appeared in various manifestations—in Tammany Hall, the Van Buren element in Jacksonian Democracy, the Barnburners, the Knights of Labor, the AFL, the CIO, and the PAC—but always they have contended with the Hamiltonian owners for the control of industry.

The other left-wing tradition is that of the agrarian radicals. They are as old as Daniel Shays, Patrick Henry, and Thomas Jefferson. They fought the Bourbons as Bentonites in Jackson's party, as Lincolnites in the Republican Party, and as Bryanites in the Democratic Party. They have been Populists, Progressives, Farmer-Laborites, and Non-Partisan Leaguers in parties of their own.

Fundamentally, the groups representing each of these four traditions is hostile to each of the others. The Hamiltonians have no use for Bourbons, Lib-Labs, or agrarians. The Bourbons are equally suspicious of right and left wing industrialists and despise the agrarian radicals. The Sons of the Wild Jackass bray at the Bourbons, kick at the Hamiltonians, and bite at the Lib-Labs. The labor groups, in turn, find their employers predatory, the Bourbons insufferable, and the agrarians intolerable.

The trick of American political tactics, of course, is to line up the representatives of three of these traditions against the fourth. The master-politicians of the past have been able to make relatively stable combinations by concentrating attention upon a common enemy. Thus Thomas Jefferson, himself a cross between an agrarian radical and a Southern planter, made an alliance with Aaron Burr's urban artisan following and fought Hamilton's Federalists. So Andrew Jackson, with Calhoun's planter aristocracy, Van Buren's laborers, and Benton's Western farmers in his train, fought the Whigs and Nick Biddle's Bank of the United States. The Republicans who put Lincoln in the White House contained agrarians from the West, workers from the East's urban centers, and industrialists of the Hamiltonian tradition. And the New Deal, under the greatest politician of them all, kept Southern Bourbons, Western agrarians, city machines, and organized labor aligned against the descendants of Alexander Hamilton.

The task before the architects of a new liberal party may be simply stated—the organization of a party which will incorporate urban progressives and agrarian radicals and will find common ground with either the Hamiltonians or the Bourbons. Whatever might be the possibility of affecting an alliance with the political employees of the NAM or the citrus growers, the ingredients for combining the agrarians and the urban Lib-Labs are lying around loose. On the industrial left the American Labor Party, the Social Democratic Federation, the Liberal Party, the Political Action Committee, and the Americans for Democratic Action have been evidences of labor's discontent. On the agricultural left there have been, in recent years, such phenomena as the Non-Partisan League in the Dakotas, the Farmer-Labor Party in Minnesota, and the Progressive Party in Wisconsin. An examination of some of these left wing movements might be enlightening.

Industrial liberal-laborism has had many manifestations in American history. Thomas Jefferson, who brought New York's workers into his party, had little use, as an agriculturist, for "urban artificers" whom he considered "panderers of vice" and the instruments through whom the liberty of the country would be overthrown. But the workers continued to gain strength and influence. By the late 1820's, a Workingman's Party appeared in Philadelphia politics with demands for mechanics lien laws, judicial reform, free public education, revision of the militia system, and opposition to banks, debtor laws, and religious legislation. Within a year the Workingmen captured a balance of power in the city council, but thereafter, under the assaults of the old parties, the movement declined.

In New York in 1829 a Labor Party with a similar program had greater success—even electing one member of the state assembly. To the delight of Tammany, which had always professed to represent the workers' interests, the new party split into three groups: the Agrarians, who took their creed from Tom Paine's writings; the State Guardianship Party, which concentrated on demands for governmental regulation; and the North American Hotel Party, which opposed public education and governmental control. As the movement split, Tammany Hall incorporated enough of the workers' demands to regain labor's support for the Democrats, and the workers' parties became the nucleus for the Van Buren faction of the party of Jackson.

From time to time workers' parties appeared again in

New York and other Eastern cities. In 1836 the Equal Rights Party, combining urban artificers and up-state "Loco-Foco" Democrats, ran candidates for New York state offices. But again, despite promising beginnings, the movement was lost in fusion and the members went off in various directions. Not for 30 years did labor emerge again into politics. Then, in 1866, the National Labor Union, incorporating as many conflicting reform organizations as the modern PAC, appeared. In 1872, as the Labor Reform Party, it ran a candidate for President, suffered defeat, and collapsed.

Four years later its leaders supported the Greenback Party, and by 1878 they had effected a merger under the label of the Greenback Labor Party. But labor was a junior partner in the combination, and although the party polled over a million votes and elected 14 Congressmen, the workers drifted away. In 1880, with an Iowan as its Presidential candidate, the party was a farmers' party, and labor turned once more to the attempt to gain its ends by economic measures.

Not until the New Deal did labor return to the political arena with a distinct party. In the interval the Socialist Labor, the Socialist, and the Communist Parties made futile bids for labor's support. But the AFL clung tenaciously to the Gompers' doctrine of disdaining partisanship and only rewarding friends and punishing enemies of labor. The exception—when the AFL and the Railroad Brotherhoods supported Bob LaFollette in 1924—only proved the rule. But as the New Deal injected new life into the labor movement and the CIO arose to challenge the AFL, the American Labor Party made its timid appearance.

As originally constituted, the American Labor Party was composed in part of the Social Democratic faction which split from the Socialists, and in part of CIO and independent unions anxious for a more active part in politics. Its major reason for existence was to be found in Franklin Roosevelt's tendency to sway to the right. The ALP, drawing in liberals who could not stomach the Hunkerism and Hagueism of the old-line Democrats, hoped to draw Roosevelt to the left. In city elections the party supported the New Deal Republican Fiorello LaGuardia, and in state and national elections it has been a leftish satellite of the Democrats. In 1936 it polled 275,000 votes for Roosevelt in the Presidential election, and by 1938 it brought 420,000 to the polls for Herbert Lehman and accounted for the slight margin of his victory over Thomas E. Dewey. But in neither case was there convincing evidence that the party drew votes which would not have gone to the Democrats anyway.

Probably the American Labor Party's only effect on politics was in making the Communist infiltration into the Democratic Party somewhat easier. Certainly it did not keep its hero from moving toward the right. In fact, as a mere satellite of the Democrats, the party has been a convenient agent in swinging labor into ardent support of the Administration's program. As the ALP lost its liberal significance and became increasingly a fellow-traveling outfit, the Social Democrats and other anti-Communist but pro-war and pro-Roosevelt elements formed a new satellite party—the Liberal Party. But in 1944 the Liberals, too, supported Roosevelt and the Democratic ticket.

The insistence of the ALP, the Liberal Party, and the PAC that Roosevelt was still a liberal effectively prevented any independent action among the Lib-Labs. Still half-wedded to Gompers' dogmas, they repudiated any suggestion

that they cooperate with such unorthodox political movements as the Farmer-Labor Party, Lemke's Union Party,
LaFollette's National Progressives, or the Michigan Commonwealth Federation. All efforts to entice the timid, de-
pendent Lib-Labs from the Democratic Party met indignant
rejection.

Fundamentally, of course, the Lib-Labs are right. Labor's
ties with industrial capital are closer than they are with
agrarian radicalism. Labor's quarrel with management is
only a dispute over the division of the spoils of industry.
The farmers are at war against the whole industrial system.
The demands of workers have been for protection and
security within the capitalist system. The agrarian radicals,
on the other hand, have fought monopoly, denounced the
banking system, and insisted upon public regulation of industry.

The orientation of agrarian radicals and urban Lib-Labs
has been completely different, and although they may have
united, from time to time, against a common enemy, they
have not felt that they had basic common interests. The
makers of an indigenous third party must dig below super-
ficial economic levels to find a base for a new political
alignment in the common humanity of workers and farmers
alike. Unless they agree upon such a base, they will find
that the timid lion of labor is afraid to lie down with Mary's
little lamb.

# CHAPTER SIX

# THE AGRARIAN REVOLT

During the twentieth century, while local workers' parties in the liberal tradition have been mere satellites of the major parties, a number of farmers' parties have given new expression to the traditions of agrarian radicalism. The Populist heritage has not been limited to Bryanism among Democrats, insurgency and progressivism among Republicans, or even the rural Western support of Socialism. It has manifested itself even more vigorously in the Non-Partisan League, the Farmer-Labor Party, and the Progressive Party in the Middle Western states.

Although each of these parties gave lip-service to the idea of farmer-labor unity and each, in varying degree, had some success in attracting labor support, their histories demonstrate the difficulty in finding a common basis for cooperation between urban liberals and agrarian radicals. In fact, each of these farmer movements was anti-industrial, and their support of "socialistic" programs—state ownership, public regulation, cooperatives—was designed to prevent industry, whether laborite or capitalistic, from strangling the farmers.

The Non-Partisan League was the oldest of these Middle Western farmers' parties—though it always carefully refrained from assuming a party name. It originated in the wheat-fields of North Dakota where the growers of spring wheat had serious grievances against the millers and grain elevators. In 1912 and 1914 the voters of North Dakota approved the erection of state grain elevators, but the legislature, owned by Minneapolis millers, ignored the popular mandate. Early in 1915 a protesting delegation of farmers heard one of their legislators tell them to "go home and slop the hogs."

Instead of complying with this sarcastic advice, Arthur C. Townley, who had failed in farming after pioneering in flax-raising in Dakota, started out with "an idea, a Ford, and $16" to form the Farmers' Non-Partisan League. Townley proposed that the League should capture the Republican primaries and choose legislators pledged to a program of state owned and operated mills and elevators, state hail insurance, laws to guarantee fair grading of grain, easier rural credits, and exemption of farm improvements from taxation. This was not socialism: it was state ownership to forestall industrial exploitation!

In 1916 the Non-Partisan League elected Lynn Frazier governor and captured the lower house of the North Dakota legislature. By 1919 it controlled the state senate as well, and had revised the constitution to permit state ownership. The legislature created an industrial commission, formed the Bank of North Dakota, and established public granaries and flour mills. It created a home-building association, a state hail insurance corporation, exempted farm improvements from taxation, and enacted a graduate income tax. For the benefit of labor the legislature enacted an eight-hour day law for women and passed a workmen's compensation act.

From the beginning the Non-Partisan League enrolled members in other states, and by 1920 it had 230,000 members in the Dakotas, Minnesota, Wisconsin, and the states of the Great Plains. Through the World War the League spread—despite its lack of concern for making the world safe for democracy and the eagerness of its opponents to charge Townley and other leaders with treason. In the early 20's, the League declined. The depression which swept the wheat country brought hardship to North Dakota's State Mill and Elevator and carried down the Home Owners Loan Association and the Bank Deposits Guarantee Act. The Bank of North Dakota, however, weathered the storm and in 1947 reported assets of over $87 million. The State Mill and Elevator recovered, too, and in 1947 it made a net operating profit of $805,000. The Home Owners Loan Association and the Bank Deposits Guarantee Act furnished precedent and example for the New Deal's more successful FHA and FDIC.

Throughout the years of the New Deal and the subsequent reaction, the Non-Partisan League suffered set-backs. However, it continues to maintain organizations in every county of North Dakota, has an active state headquarters in Bismarck, and publishes *The Leader* each week. In 1946 it endorsed and helped send Republicans William Langer to the U. S. Senate and Charles R. Robertson to the House of Representatives. In North Dakota, the League recently elected three state officers, and it now holds 51 out of 113 seats in the lower house of the legislature and 19 of the 49 senate seats. By 1948 the Non-Partisan League was stronger in the state than it had been for a decade.

As League influence declined outside North Dakota, the Farmer-Labor Party took its place. In 1919 a hopeless remnant of the progressive movement formed a Committee of Forty-Eight, and called a national conference for St. Louis in December. Three hundred harassed delegates— threatened with reactionary lawlessness and patriotic vio-

lence and only protected by a court injunction which permitted them to meet—drafted a platform favoring public
ownership of transportation facilities, equal rights, restora-
tion of free speech and assembly, abolition of injunctions in
labor disputes, and a popular referendum on war. It opposed militarism and military training, and demanded the
Government take the lead in securing international agreement for disarmament.

In July 1920 a national convention, called by the St.
Louis conference, met in Chicago, but it could not agree on
either platform or candidates. Labor delegates, however,
bolted from the meeting and launched the Farmer-Labor
Party with Parley P. Christensen of Utah as its candidate.
The party did poorly in the national elections, but a dis-
senting branch succeeded in capturing Minnesota—and
thereafter the Farmer-Labor Party dominated the Gopher
State.

Perhaps because it was a local party, the Farmer-Labor
Party succeeded for a time in keeping both its wings in line.
It sent Henrik Shipstead to the Senate in 1922 and in a
special election in 1923 it sent a "dirt farmer," Magnus
Johnson, to join him. In 1924 it supported LaFollette.
In Congress its representatives joined the farm bloc against
Coolidge, Hoover, and Mellon. At home, so long as the
AFL controlled the labor movement in the Twin Cities, the
Farmer-Labor movement was essentially an expression of
agrarian demands.

The situation changed, however as labor grew more important in the state. The depression invigorated the labor
wing of the party, and the organization of the truck drivers
by the Trotskyite Dunne brothers brought a shift in state
issues from rural to urban concerns. No longer did farmers'

grievances seem so important, while the open shop became a matter of vital significance.

For a half-dozen years Gov. Floyd Olson managed to maintain a balance between the militant laborers and the Farm Holiday Association which had combined to support him. Elected in 1930, he was reelected in 1932 and 1934. His death in 1936 loosed the only personal ties which bound farmers and laborers together.

Olson's successor, Elmer Benson, lacked the political and personal qualities to hold his followers. The elements of the party split apart in personal struggles for leadership. Hjalmar Petersen led the farmers against Benson—and eventually led them back into the Republican Party. By 1938 Shipstead had returned to the Republican fold and shortly thereafter began a losing fight with Harold Stassen for control of Republican policy in Minnesota.

Meantime Benson, losing farmer support, drew closer to the Communist-dominated CIO unions in the labor wing. In 1944 the Farmer-Labor Party joined the Democrats in a new coalition and barely succeeded in carrying the state for Franklin D. Roosevelt. In the first years of World War II, the Tobin interests drove the Trotskyites out of the Minneapolis truck drivers' union and railroaded their leaders to jail for treason. The war brought increased industrial activity to the Twin Cities, and the Communists secured their hold on new CIO unions. By 1946 the Democratic-Farmer-Labor coalition was torn between hunker Democrats, Communists, and a non-Communist liberal wing while the farmers who had once been the backbone of the movement were swamped under by the Stassen brand of Republicans.

A situation similar in many essentials, but differing in its form, overtook the Progressive Party of Wisconsin. For long years the Badger state was a one-party state where the Democrats had never been important. There the Progressives had long functioned as the party of the primaries, opposing the conservatives among the Republicans for control of the GOP. In general the Progressives, successfully marshalled by Old Bob, Young Bob, and Phil LaFollette, controlled the rural districts while the Victor Berger-Dan Hoan Socialists—who were "gutter Socialists" in the eyes of Eastern doctrinaires—controlled Milwaukee and had influence along the industrial shores of Lake Michigan.

For a generation the Progressives acted as a leaven within the Republican Party, yet after 1920 they never supported a Republican Presidential nominee. With the inauguration of Roosevelt, the Progressives reaped their reward by sharing the patronage with the state's reactionary Democrats. The anomalous situation came to an end in 1934. As a distinctly left of center party, the Progressives withdrew from the Republican fold and began an independent existence by nominating Phil for the governorship and Bob for the U. S. Senate. The new Progressive Party proved its strength by electing both the LaFollette brothers.

Phil came to suspect both the methods and the intent of President Roosevelt. Moreover, as Roosevelt shifted his foreign policy, the Progressive leaders refused to follow suit. Traditionally opposed to foreign war, and reflecting well the dominant sentiment of the Middle West, the Progressives proclaimed every "step short of war" a stride towards fascism and imperialism.

Reelected in 1936 for a third term as governor, Phil displayed an impatience to get ahead with reforms in the government. His opponents, both from the New Deal and from the Republicans, were quick to turn the well-developed techniques of a "smear campaign" upon him.

In the erroneous belief that the liberals of the country were as disgusted as he with the half-way measures of the Democrats, Phil LaFollette launched the National Progressives of America. Rooseveltians, Communists, and Republicans, in accord for once, professed to see a fascist swastika in the party's symbol—a voter's X in a circle! Then a LaFollette-dominated board of regents ousted Glenn Frank from the presidency of the University of Wisconsin, and Frank, with a far better nose for publicity than the bumbling regents, got the breaks in the press and proclaimed himself a martyr to LaFolletism.

Finally, towards the end of his third term, Phil called the legislature into special session and forced through a series of basic governmental reforms—most of which were efforts to modernize state administration. The howls from the Old Guard were immediate, loud, and vicious, and the Socialist Party and the Trotskyites, each of whom had advocated, in times past, the same reforms, promptly proclaimed the governor a dangerous man.

In 1938 Phil was swept out of office in the general wave of reaction that removed Benson in Minnesota and Frank Murphy in Michigan. The victorious Republicans promptly slashed at the reforms enacted under the Progressives. By 1942, however, the voters were tired of the inept clowning of Gov. Julius ("the Just") Heil, Milwaukee capitalist, and a Progressive won the governorship. The governor-elect died before taking office, and his successor turned out to be an honest Republican. The election of 1942, however, sent only six Progressives to the state senate and 13 to the assembly.

This marked the collapse of the Progressive Party. It had suffered from defection to the New Deal. William T. Evjue, editor of Madison's virile *Capital Times* and one of the founders of the Progressive Party, and Dan Hoan, long-time Socialist mayor of Milwaukee, abandoned the Progressives to insist that all "liberals" must unite behind Roosevelt regardless of the long-range consequences. The party suffered from the war, which took the young voters who had been the party's most active workers.

In this situation, the party had three lines of action open to it. It could join the Democrats, as Evjue, Hoan, and a handful of Federal office-holders proposed, and become the liberal wing of that party in the state. It could return to the Republicans from which it had sprung and resume the ancient battle of the primaries with the Stalwarts. Or, in the third place, it could remain separate in the state and try to become the nucleus for a national party. In 1946, despairing of achieving the latter, and no longer able to draw support from the labor movement—already heavily infested with Communists—the party formally disbanded and reentered the Republican ranks.

Once again, fusion took its accustomed toll. Senator LaFollette failed to win renomination in the primaries, and only two former Progressives, now Republicans, returned to Congress.

With the collapse of the Progressive Party in Wisconsin and the hopeless division of the Farmer-Labor Party in Minnesota, there disappeared the last organized groups which could conceivably have led a movement for a genuine national party of liberals.

# CHAPTER SEVEN

# THE REPUBLICAN PAST

Among the ranks of Republicans one may find some re-
tired Progressives who assert, when prodded by their con-
sciences into wishful rationalizations, that the party of
Lincoln, Theodore Roosevelt, Bob LaFollette, and George
Norris can become a liberal party. To prove their point,
these unhappy relics of a faded past cite the long history
of high ideals the Republican Party has professed.

Strange though it may seem after 90 years of the party's
history, the Republican "progressives" are right in asserting
that their party began as a liberal movement. By the
1850's, the Democratic Party, repudiating its Jacksonian
background, had supplanted the Whigs as the political
dwelling-place of the nation's conservatives. Its dominant
element was the South's planter-aristocracy, with whom, in
close alliance, were the financial and commercial groups of
the Eastern seaboard.

Against this combination, the militant Republicans began
a liberal crusade.

In 1854, when the Democrats proposed to open the
Western territories to slavery, a mass-meeting in Ripon,
Wisconsin, solemnly resolved to "throw old party organizations to the winds and organize a new party on the sole basis
of the non-extension of slavery." When the Kansas-Nebraska Bill passed, the "Free Democrats" of Michigan called
for a mass convention "springing from thousands, irrespec-
tive of political organization."

On July 13, anniversary of the Northwest Ordinance, opponents of the "Nebraska iniquity" assembled in Madison, Indianapolis, Columbus, and even Montpelier, and a few weeks later in Illinois, New York, and Iowa. All pledged themselves to return the nation to free principles, excluding slavery from the territories, and repealing the hated Fugitive Slave Act.

The Republican movement, beginning in "grass-roots" mass-meetings, was launched without the assistance of professional politicians. Lesser politicos, many of them fugitives from the dying Whig Party, and some of them renegade Democrats, joined the movement, but no one of them dominated it.

Like the Populists of a later day, the Republicans had no Hamilton or Jefferson, no Jackson, Debs, LaFollette, or Roosevelt in the role of peerless leader and indispensable man. Republican orators in years to come would make much of Abraham Lincoln, but the Illinois politician stayed clear of the movement for two full years, and even after he joined the rising party, he was not its leader. His canonization came only after his death.

In the beginning, the Republican Party was a coalescence of diverse groups. Some of them were liberal, fiercely devoted to the rights of men and hating slavery as a devil's creation. Among them were the Free-Soilers, who had been Barnburning, Loco-foco Democrats in the days of Andrew Jackson and Martin Van Buren.

There were anti-Nebraska Democrats who had left the planter-ridden Democracy only after Stephen A Douglas' Kansas-Nebraska Bill threatened to open the territories to slavery.

There were abolitionists—Liberty Party men—a move-

ment first begun as a crusade against slavery when Charles
G. Finney evangelized a stolid Calvinism.

There were Temperance men, eager to battle the rum-
soaked Democracy and extend the benefits of a "Maine
Law" to the nation.

There were remnants of Utopian Socialism—Brook
Farm, New Harmony, and the Phalanxes—the "long-
haired men and short-haired women" who had advocated
Women's Rights. And there were the Grahamites, vege-
tarians, hydro-therapists, and spiritualists.

And there were the workers from Pittsburgh, Philadelphia, and New York who supported a protective tariff
which would shield free American laborers from cheap
foreign competition.

It was no wonder that the respectable planters and
financiers recoiled from the early Republicans—a party
that was, in the words of its Democratic critics, "committed
to Socialism and Communism—to no private property, no
church, no laws, no government—to free love, free lands,
free women, and free churches."

But these elements did not attract sufficient popular
support to carry an election. Before 1860, the anti-slavery
forces had been joined by other elements who were less
concerned with the rights of man but who were equally
opposed to the Democrats. The Whig Party, heir to Hamiltonian Federalism and exponent of the "American System"
of internal improvements, protective tariff, and a national
bank, disintegrated after 1852 and its displaced personnel
sought a new home among the Republicans.

The Know-Nothing Party, devoted to religious bigotry,
recruited briefly among the erstwhile Whigs, and then dis-
solved. Its members and its office-hopeful hacks attached

themselves to the new party. From Pennsylvania came the People's Party, whose name belied its industrialist principles, but whose leaders, like the corruptionist Simon Cameron and the predatory Thad Stevens, could weep copiously over the plight of the slave whenever an oratorical tear could profit their railroads, factories, or mines.

The groups who were devoted to the rights of man and those promoting the rights of property had so little in common that the early Republican Party could not formulate its principles. In 1856 the party platform stood firmly against slavery and polygamy—the "twin relics of barbarism"—in the territories, but it could not find agreement among its clashing members on any other vital problem. Its Presidential candidate was John C. Fremont, a novice in politics whose glamorized record as an explorer gave him claim to the fanciful title "Pathfinder of the West." Lacking any national cohesion, the party became a series of state parties, each fighting the Democrats on local issues.

For the first five years of their party's existence, 1855-1860, the Republicans devoted their efforts to building state organizations. One by one, they gained a foothold in the Northern states, and in the process one or the other of the wings of the party gained ascendancy in each state. In New England, outside Massachusetts, and in New York, the Republican Party was only the old, conservative Whig Party in a new anti-slavery garb. In Massachusetts and in most of the Western states, the radical elements—enlisting small farmers by promises of a homestead law—were dominant. In Pennsylvania and New Jersey, the industrialists had control. In each state, the divergent groups had effected compromises among themselves. In general the compromises consisted in superimposing the humanitarian slogans of the liberal groups upon the economic program of the conservative elements.

By 1860, the Republican Party had sufficient strength in the states to win—thanks, in part, to the Democratic split— the Presidential election. Its platform in that year, however, bore evidence that the liberal elements had been willing to settle for fair words. The party was still opposed to the extension of slavery, still rampant against polygamy, and in favor of a homestead bill ("Vote yourself a farm" was a popular appeal) and Federal aid to agricultural education. These items—together with an endorsement of the Declaration of Independence which barely passed the Chicago convention—satisfied the liberals.

The rest of the platform promised Federal aid for a Pacific railroad, endorsed a tariff in language that Pennsylvania's industrialists could use in the campaign, and favored river and harbor improvement. The words were the words of Jefferson: the program stemmed from Alexander Hamilton. On this ambidextrous platform the party selected an old-time Whig who repudiated abolitionism but who was agile enough to ride two horses into the troubled stream of politics.

Lincoln's election precipitated the secession of the South, and secession and civil war proved a god-send to the discordant Republicans. Under Lincoln's skillful direction, the party shifted its program from opposition to slavery extension to the preservation of the union. Super-patriotism became thereafter a basic ingredient of Republicanism and for a generation after the war Republican orators rallied the voters about the flag, "waved the bloody shirt" of Civil War issues, appealed for patriots to save the Union at the ballot boxes, and denounced all Democrats ("Scratch a

Democrat and you'll find a rebel under his skin"; "Maybe all Democrats aren't rebels, but all rebels are Democrats") as disguised Confederates.

The exigencies of war and the patriotic necessity of saving the Union enabled the Republicans to use the military to win elections. In 1862 the Army's control of the border states kept the Republican majority in Congress. In 1864 the soldiers' vote, military supervision of the polls in the border states, and arbitrary military arrests of Democrats insured Lincoln's reelection. For the next decade the military occupation of the South enabled the Republicans to garner the Negro vote and retain control of the national Government. For 20 years the Republicans controlled the Government without once winning a clear majority of free uncontrolled voters.

To these developments the liberal, humanitarian elements in the Republican Party gave, in general, their approval. They could not cavil at a war to save the Union—and the pacifist groups like the American Peace Society and pacifist leaders like Charles Sumner found verbal formulae ("This war is different"; "We oppose international war, not civil war") to support the war effort. The abolitionist groups supported the war because it was freeing the slaves—although they were thoroughly unhappy over the inadequate Emancipation Proclamation—and after the war they continued in the party because it promised Negro equality. Even after 1876, when the Republicans sold the Negro back to the Bourbon Southerners in exchange for the Presidency, the hearts of Republican orators bled for the Negro and the race issue kept the honest humanitarians in line. The Free-Soil and small farming groups, who could not be bought with words, got a Homestead Act and the Morrill

Land Grant for agricultural education—and these were the only tangible benefits to the liberal wing of the GOP.

But behind the liberal facade of Union-saving, slave-freeing, and Negro rights, the big-business groups of Republicans erected the solid bulwarks of economic conservatism. In the midst of the war, and under the excuse of emergency, they donated huge areas of the public domain and vast amounts of public credit to the Union Pacific and other railroads. They raised the tariff to levels beyond the wildest dreams of Alexander Hamilton. They created the National Bank system, and after the war, they paid off the bondholders, who bought bonds with inflated greenbacks, in gold and they put the country, through the "crime of '73," solidly on the gold standard.

By the 1870's the Republican Party, which had begun as a liberal movement and had fought the largest single capital interest in the country, had become the party of conservative capitalism. From Grant to Hoover, the party was the party of Big Business and the Trusts, of superpatriotism and imperialism, of national banks, high tariff, the gold standard, and low wages. By 1930 its original liberalism had faded beyond recognition.

From time to time, however, the original liberal elements in Republicanism raised voices against the conservative dominance. The record of Republican insurgency is long, and not without its triumphs. In 1864 the abolitionists tried to split away and run Fremont for President. In 1872 free-traders, civil-service advocates, and opponents of restrictive reconstruction measures broke away and formed the Liberal Republican Party. But the movement proved abortive. Sorehead politicians, dissatisfied over patronage distribution but with no interest in reform, got control of the new party.

By 1876 the Liberal Republicans were back in the fold, but they continued as "Mugwumps" to annoy the "Stalwarts." They succeeded in forcing civil service reform on the party, and later in enacting anti-trust legislation. They inspired the trust-busting of Theodore Roosevelt and the tariff insurgency of the elder LaFollette. From the ranks of Republican liberals came the original impetus for the Bull Moosers of 1912 and the Progressives of 1924. Among their leaders have been Albert J. Beveridge, Joseph L. Bristow, John P. Dolliver, Victor Murdoch, Robert M. LaFollette, Jr., William E. Borah, and George W. Norris.

Most of these Republican progressives have come out of the Middle West, and most of them represent the original, agrarian elements which entered into the Republican Party. To these "Sons of the Wild Jackass," and to the reform movement they have supported, the progressive Republican leaders can point with pride. But whether they support the argument that the Republican Party can become a liberal vehicle is an open question. To that question must be brought the record of the Republicans as the party of opposition during the days of the New Deal, the second World War, and the current period.

# CHAPTER EIGHT

# THE REPUBLICAN PRESENT

The sweeping success of the Republican Party in 1946 was not a victory for any clear-cut philosophy. It did not mean that either the agrarian liberals of the party nor the reactionaries had won control of the organization. In the Congressional elections of 1946 the most potent slogan was "Had Enough? Vote Republican." The voters, who had clearly had enough, took revenge on the Democrats, but when they voted Republican they endorsed no special program. The Republican Party had failed to formulate such a program.

For 14 years of the New Deal and the second World War, the GOP was characterized by confusion, incredulity, acquiescence, and hopeful expectancy. Divided among themselves, bearing the odium of having been in power when the Great Depression came, the Republicans had been unable to capture the spotlight from the Democrats' dramatic leaders. Young men left the Republican ranks, and seasoned hacks sought office by offering to out-New Deal the Democrats. Confronted by the improvident improvisations of the New Deal, Republicans sounded alarms, pointed fingers of warning, and engaged in all the other cliches of partisan oratory, but they never offered a plausible substitute.

The Republican failure to formulate a program sprang naturally from the party's internal confusions. These confusions had been apparent in the glorious '20s, when the party had complete power. Then the dominant philosophy of the party had been the Big Business dogma that America had entered a "New Economic Era."

In this new era, bankers and preachers and college professors told the people that old economic ideas could be discarded. Henry Ford condemned saving, and Thomas A. Edison, repudiating the doctrines of Benjamin Franklin, ridiculed the idea of thrift. From the pundits of the New Economic Era, Americans learned that depressions and poverty were obsolete, that the entire nation—as the wide spread of stock-holdings proved—was becoming capitalistic, that stock-market speculation was a sign of exuberant health, that high money rates were desirable, and that the valuation of stocks did not have to depend on a company's earnings or prospects.

These were weird doctrines. In the midst of their sway there arrived in the United States a little French druggist who had a prescription for happiness. All that was needed, proclaimed M. Coue, was to repeat the formula, "Day by day, in every way, I'm getting better and better."

The formula fitted perfectly into the optimistic mood of the New Economic Era. Big Business and the Republicans —Harding, Coolidge and Hoover—envisioned a capitalistic world in which the factory wheels kept turning, where, day by day, more and more goods were produced, and where, in every way, men lived in better houses, rode in constantly improved automobiles, and listened to better and better tunes over steadily improving radios. There were to be two better cars in every garage, and the two chickens in the pot were to be fatter than ever before.

It was unfortunate for the Republicans that their incantations of the Coue formula could not alter the facts of economic life. The problems before the nation—farm collapse, crime, waterpower control, the veterans bonus, international peace, prohibition, and unemployment—would not evaporate before the magic words of M. Coue, Henry Ford, Andy Mellon, Thomas Edison, or Calvin Coolidge.

Again insurgency raised its ugly head—as it often had done in the Republican past. This time it was led by George Norris and Bob LaFollette, Jr., and was supported by the Farm Bloc. The insurgents demanded remedial legislation for farmers, and they blocked Hoover on tariff and waterpower legislation. "Sons of the Wild Jackass" they were—and they were clear demonstrations that not even the fatuous Coueism of the New Economic Era was accepted by all Republicans.

The factional divisions among the Republicans prevented the party from making a coherent assault upon the Great Depression. In 1930, they lost control of the House of Representatives, and two years later, completely confused and discredited, they lost the Presidency, the Senate, and most of their state organizations. By 1936 the party had reached the lowest level of its history. Its candidate, Alfred Landon, polled only the electoral votes of Maine and Vermont.

By this time the Republican Party was down to bed rock. Only the true-blue, dyed-in-the-wool, birth-right Republicans were left. Those who had merely come along for the ride had long since jumped on the Roosevelt bandwagon. But not even then was the Republican Party united. In 1938, the Republicans gained some successes, and Gallup polls, reflecting the growing weariness with the New Deal, indicated a faint possibility of national success in 1940. But the old confusions began. The party could not decide whether it was to be liberal, conservative, or middle-of-the-road. Senator Arthur Vandenberg of Michigan favored a conservative coalition with "Jeffersonian" Democrats. Others wanted an honest tory position. Still others hoped to steal liberal thunder and pose as reformed New Dealers.

Throughout these years, the major attitude of the party was incredulity, and its major action was acquiescence. In 1932 Republicans could not believe that the majority of the voters, with the stern eye of the Almighty watching them in the polling booths, could mark the Democratic column. They were equally incredulous in 1933 when the banks closed and opened again. They were amazed as the NRA began to operate, and the multiplied agencies to "fix and freeze" took shape. To each in turn the Republicans dutifully expressed partisan opposition, but they found that the voters were deaf to all warnings. In 1936, the Liberty League made the incredible discovery that the crack in the Liberty Bell was no longer a symbol to arouse the nation.

In the end, the Republicans began to spend their time watching the clock—but they always thought it was later than it was. Time alone, they came to believe, would work in their favor. In 1936 the Republican theme song was "Three Long Years." In 1940 they were incredulous that the people would approve a third term. In 1944, Candidate Dewey's major plea was that the men of the New Deal were old and tired. In 1939, Delbert Clark, writing in the *New York Times,* summed up the basic Republican hope:

"There has never been a Democratic administration since the Civil War that did not eventually hand the country back to the Republicans on a silver platter, and there is considerable chance that this one will not break the precedent. The Democratic Party, a queer, hybrid creature for the past half century or more, pulls itself together now and then and follows a peerless leader to victory, but eventually the old dogfights between liberal and conservative break out again, and up pop the Republicans."

But in the meantime, until the people had had enough to vote Republican, the Grand Old Party acquiesced in the New Deal's accomplishments. Despite opposition and despite their Cassandra-prophecies of doom, the Republicans endorsed the SEC, the Social Security Act, the FHA, the CCC, the FDIC, the Maritime Commission, and the Civil Aeronautics Authority. They denounced Democratic methods and charged the New Deal with graft, waste, and incompetence, but promised only to take over the machine and run it more honestly.

The worst display of Republican confusion and acquiescence came as the Democratic Administration pursued its efforts to enter World War II. No sooner had Britain declared war on Hitler, than President Roosevelt called for repeal of the Neutrality Act. Promptly the Republicans voiced opposition. "This is not our war," proclaimed Senator Vandenberg. "It need not—it should not—become our war." Yet, at the same time, the Michigan Senator promised to "unite wholeheartedly with the President . . . and present an impregnably united front to the entire world."

Such words were the voice of a "loyal opposition," and gave the President no pause. He met more opposition from Democratic Senator Burton K. Wheeler than from the Republicans. They acquiesced in the repeal of the neutrality laws, in the destroyer deal, in Lend-Lease—in all the "steps short of war."

For liberals looking for a political vehicle, the Republican record of 14 years of inconsequential opposition, of time serving, of confusion, amazement, and acquiescence offers little hope. Even more disgusting, however, than the record of things done is the realization of things undone. Through the long years of their opposition, the Republicans ignored two elements in their own tradition which might, had they been developed, have furnished a sound alternative to the New Deal. And they might, too, have offered some hope to the sound liberal elements of the land.

The first of these was the tradition of improving the machinery of democracy. The progressive elements, both in and out of the Republican Party, had long been concerned with increasing the area of democracy. From the Civil Rights Bill of 1867 to the unicameral legislature of Nebraska, from Negro suffrage to woman suffrage, from the initiative and referendum to the popular election of Senators, the progressives devised new means to make democracy work in an age of technological change and growing economic concentration.

The New Deal increased the power of the executive, multiplied irresponsible bureaucratic agencies, and moved steadily towards the goal of "welfare" statism. Repeatedly the Republicans raised the wolf-cry of dictatorship—yet no single proposal for returning the government to the people came from them. Repeatedly the Republicans charged the New Deal with corruption—yet never did they move to reinvigorate the grand jury which had been an ancient Anglo-Saxon instrument of popular control.

Nor did the Republicans demand that the American delegation, at least, to the United Nations be popularly elected. For 14 years, while they protested against "the most gigantic bureaucracy ever known to an alleged democracy and which attempts to order the minutiae of life and livelihood from one central tyranny in Washington"—the words are Vandenberg's—the Republicans offered no democratic alternative.

The second element in the progressive tradition which the Republicans ignored was sound scholarship. For years the progressives, especially in Wisconsin, had attempted to apply the results of research to the problems of government. In the Badger State the intimate relations between the University of Wisconsin and the Capitol had effected a marriage of soil and seminar. Out of such unions, in Wisconsin and elsewhere, had come the Legislative Reference Library system, efficient public utility regulation, sound social legislation, and the "streamlining" of state governments.

This concept of governmental reform based on research instead of improved opportunism was not foreign to the Republicans. Even in the days of economic Coueism, Herbert Hoover—who cooed steadily about prosperity turning the corner—applied the methods of solid study to government's problems. He sought the facts through commissions and fearlessly—and generally tactlessly—tried to incorporate their findings into law and administration. Democrats ridiculed the commissions—and the situation clearly called for some quicker answers than research could give—but the New Deal's only sound and lasting reforms (always excepting the TVA) were based upon Hoover-inspired reports.

Herbert Hoover was neither a glamorous leader nor an apt politician, but his methods were sounder than either Republican Coueism or New Deal improvisations.

In the 14 years of their decline the Republicans might well have followed Hoover's lead, supported careful research and planning, and combined their findings with new devices for democracy. Their failure to offer a valid and democratic alternative to the New Deal, their merely partisan opposition, and their 14-year record of confusion are reflected anew in their record in the 80th Congress, where they were in control of both Houses for the first time in 17 years. The record they have made is almost wholly negative and, in many respects, downright reactionary. The fact that its program does not appeal to a nation which, by all signs, was thoroughly fed up with the Democrats, is confirmed by the latest Gallup polls.

The GOP does number some outstanding progressives—George Aiken, Wayne Morse, and Merlin Hull, to mention three now in Congress—but its record, its leadership, its "program" for the future hardly encourage liberals to call it their political home.

# CHAPTER NINE

# THE NEW DEAL PAST

The death of the New Deal was accompanied by the end of idealism which marked its earlier days. Upon its demise, its erstwhile supporters and one-time syncophants scattered in all directions. Some have become stalwart supporters of the Bourbon-machine coalition which is the Democratic Party. Others have joined the fellow-traveling fringes of totalitarianism. Some have transferred their hopes to the United Nations, and some—refusing to abandon hopes for a liberal America—work for democratic progressivism in Americans for Democratic Action or in the Committee on Education for a New Party.

To those, like the members of these latter groups, who have not abandoned hope, it must be apparent that the New Deal was in some respects a failure from the beginning. It failed, in the first place, because it was primarily a political movement—because its experiments and its expedients were designed for political effect. It did not have a consistent, uniform plan for dealing with the economic ills which generations of mismanagement and monopolistic exploitation had brought upon the nation.

But, in the second place, the New Deal failed because it departed from the fundamental concepts of the American progressive tradition. Its liberal supporters were led, first gradually and then precipitately, down a pathway which went diametrically opposite from the direction in which

Jefferson, Bryan, LaFollette, and a host of other progressives had pointed.

For long decades before the New Deal the progressive forces of America had been waging a ceaseless struggle against big-business monopoly and against the aggressions of government. As far back as the '70s and the '80s, the progressives—faced with the rising trusts, with railroad pools and extortionate rates, with public utility empires, and with the concentration of money and credit in the hands of a few financial magnates—had sought a means of protecting the people from the predatory interests who were making a mockery of the ancient dogma that America was a land of opportunity.

Faced with a declining standard of living, they had sought to protect the right of labor to organize, to strike for better wages and conditions of work, and to bargain with employers. They had sought, too, to protect women and children from exploitation by industry, and to safeguard public health from adulterated foods and poisonous drugs.

Wisely or unwisely, the progressives had turned to government to effect their ends. Recognizing that the railroads, the corporate trusts, and the financiers derived their powers from their control of the government, the liberals launched a two-fold program which would, first, restore the government to the people, and second, use the government's power for social reform.

To achieve the first objective, they supported such devices as woman suffrage, the direct election of Senators, and the initiative and the referendum.

As they worked, with necessary but discouraging slowness, towards a greater democracy and a more responsible government, the liberal forces created new agencies to control and regulate the economic empire about them. In the states they developed agencies ranging from legislative reference libraries to industrial commissions, power commissions, and banking commissions.

In the national Government, they created the Interstate Commerce Commission, the Federal Trade Commission, and passed such laws as the Sherman and Clayton Anti-Trust Acts and the Pure Food and Drug Act. In state and nation, the progressive forces sought to use a democratic government to advance the general welfare with social legislation which would equalize advantages between rich and poor, and eventually eliminate poverty from the land of plenty.

Yet the progressive movement, battling against the economic and political doctrines of *laissez faire,* never forgot that social legislation and monopoly control could only be obtained by the preservation of democracy in government and freedom for the individual. They could look abroad to central Europe—and especially Germany—where progress in social legislation was far in advance of America. But as they looked, they saw that the German system was a palliative offered by a ruling clique to prevent democratic change.

Social legislation without democracy was an opiate for the people. The system in central Europe was moving relentlessly toward state capitalism, and it was producing a swollen beaureaucracy. Moreover, the German system was accompanied by an ever-present police, by a constant interference with the life of the people, and by an oppressive military establishment. American progressives preferred the slower but more productive processes of democracy and freedom.

The progressive movement in America came to a sudden halt with the advent of the first World War. To meet the exigencies of the war, the Government adopted new administrative measures, practiced new methods of propaganda, and transformed old agencies, originally designed for democratic controls, into parts of the war machine. The nation accepted—but only for the moment—the processes and the philosophy of state capitalism. When the war ended and a postwar reaction set in, the new, war-born controls relaxed. Relaxed, too, were the restraints which the progressive movement had imposed. During the 12 years of "normalcy" which followed the war, *laissez faire* revived and progressivism lost ground.

Ostensibly and superficially, the New Deal was a return to the old progressive tradition. Actually, the return was to the methods of the World War and to the concepts of European state capitalism. Its method smacked strangely of the World War: The President declared a state of war existed against the depression and the "Blue Eagle" campaign was reminiscent of the propaganda tactics of 1917. The President enjoyed the military idiom that he used, but the resemblance to the war extended beyond language. As in the war, the monopolists were the ones who profited most. The Bourbons in agriculture reaped the benefits of the AAA, and the big industrialists, complaining of the sops thrown to labor, reveled in the power conferred by the NRA.

Steadily the New Deal moved away from the democratic freedom which had characterized the progressive tradition. Steadily it moved toward a system of compulsion. When actual war against Hitler and the Japanese supplanted the make-believe war against the depression the governmental bureaucracy called for new coercive measures against the American people.

The Government used the Army against recalcitrant corporations. It demanded a National Service Act to bring labor under the executive's control and insisted upon peacetime conscription for American youth. With these moves the Democratic Party stripped many of the last shreds of its liberalism. It had capitalized upon the progressive tradition only to abandon it and liberals began to search anew for a political party devoted to democracy.

# CHAPTER TEN

# THE NEW DEAL PRESENT

Long before the death of Franklin Roosevelt it had become apparent that the New Deal, which had made itself attractive with third party cosmetics, had ceased to be a vehicle for progressivism. "Dr. New Deal," in the leader's own words, was replaced by Colonel Win D. Wahr. After Roosevelt's death, the accession of Missouri politicos, the departure of the Old Curmudgeon and of "Corn" Wallace—who gardened in Madison Square—and the eventual announcement of the "Truman Doctrine" gave successive confirmations that the New Deal, upon which the liberals had once pinned their hopes, had gone forever.

But, now that the New Deal is past history, those liberals who are torturing their minds about the political future of the nation might learn something from recent history. A brief review of the 1930's should throw light upon some of the tendencies of the 1940's. It might, for example, give perspective to tendencies of the Government to degenerate into machine politics, for liberals to seek refuge in Stalinism, and for onetime idealists to forsake principles for the transient rewards of political "realism."

Any evaluation of the New Deal must of course, start with the Great Depression. The New Deal began at a moment when the banks of the land had collapsed, millions were out of work, industry was stagnant, and farmers were bankrupt in the midst of an unmarketable surplus. The new President brought to these problems a voice, at once reassuring and courageous, and his associates in Brain Trust and Congress began a dramatic series of acts whose vigor, contrasting sharply with Mr. Hoover's cautious moves, captured the popular imagination.

Examining the record of the first months of the New Deal, any evaluation will give full credit to the positive achievements of the President and the New Dealers. It will recognize that the relief program was immediately necessary to save the human victims of economic collapse from freezing and starvation. It will recognize that the public works sponsored by the New Deal added elements of beauty and utility to the American scene. Moreover, the Tennessee Valley Authority and the Labor Relations Acts made profound improvements in the utilization of natural resources and in human relations.

But as any honest evaluation of the New Deal must catalogue these and other positive achievements of the Roosevelt administration, it must also answer this basic question:

What social or economic philosophy inspired or infused the New Deal?

First of all, it seems evident, there was more political motivation than economic philosophy in the New Deal's economic program. In the beginning, amid a running patter of "relief, recovery, and reform," the New Dealers pulled rabbits out of their hat with fascinating rapidity. There was—faster almost than the eye could follow—the banking moratorium and the Emergency Banking Act, the Economy Bill, the repeal of Prohibition, the CCC, the NRA, the AAA, the CWA, the FERA, the PWA, and the WPA.

For a time, these measures bemused the populace into thinking the New Deal was a revolution, and the agonized howls of the more reactionary "economic royalists" lent support to the thought. But all too soon it became apparent that "Dr. New Deal" was a homeopath, alleviating symptoms but avoiding any treatment which would reach the cause of the nation's ills.

The causes of the Great Depression, which should have been treated, lay deep in the economic and social system. Fundamentally, the capitalist system was producing an ever-increasing gap between the small group of owners and the great mass of laborers and consumers. A disproportionate part of the national income went to pay managers, investors, and the financiers, while the laboring and the salaried classes, constituting four-fifths of the population, received less than 40% of the total income of the land.

The savings of the small upper-income groups went into new capital—into factories, banks, and trade—increasing the productive capacity of the country far beyond the ability of the consuming groups to absorb the products. More goods could be produced than ever before, but fewer people could purchase them. The land fared ill when wealth accumulated and men decayed.

Partly as a result of Federal Reserve policies, and partly because of the increasing concentration of wealth, monopolies had grown stronger, and, by various devices, were controlling prices, regulating and limiting production, and dominating capital investments. Monopolistic price-fixing prevented adjustments in accordance with classical principles of supply and demand. Price-fixing brought less demand and diminished production; smaller production brought less employment; more unemployment made for a still smaller demand—not only for the goods of the monopolies, but for the products of the farm and the services of men.

The total situation demanded a drastic overhauling of the entire American economic system. If it were overhauled with capitalism preserved, the logical and inevitable process would involve putting business and finance "through the wringer" of bankruptcy. This had been the method of previous depressions: debts had been liquidated, everyone had "taken a step down," and then new demand and new credit had brought new production. The business cycle began to turn again in its accustomed orbit towards a new depression.

But if the overhauling were to take place on another level—if we were to admit that the capitalist economy led inevitably to recurring disaster—the process would be equally drastic. It would involve national planning after careful study. It would involve public ownership of railroads and utilities, and public regulation of capital and credit. It would involve reorienting the popular mind to consider the public welfare more important than private profits.

Either of these approaches would have involved dealing with the causes of economic collapse and social disintegration. Either would have involved adjusting all parts of the national economy into a new system. Either, too, would have involved dangers, and either would have required a high order of courage. But either approach would have been an attempt to cure the causes of the depression.

The New Dealers either did not understand the problem or did not dare tackle it. At the moment of Franklin Roosevelt's inauguration, the populace was in a mood to have followed readily along any road he led. The people welcomed the revolution they believed he was promoting.

But Roosevelt was not sponsoring revolution. "What we seek is balance in our economic system," he proclaimed,

"—balance between agriculture and industry and balance between the wage earner, the employer, and the consumer." And the devices he sought to use were price-fixing and patchwork repairs. "Fix and freeze" became the watchwords of the New Deal—became the homeopathic remedies with which the President, yielding to each pressure group as it arose, sought to treat the deep-seated diseases of the economic body.

The first evidence that the New Deal was no revolution came with the Emergency Banking and Gold Control Act of March 9, 1933, and the Banking Act of 1933. The President's primary concern—as he stated it to Congress, was the "opening of banks for the resumption of business." The acts increased the powers of the Federal Reserve Board. The Federal Reserve System remained in the hands of the bankers, and the Federal Deposit Insurance Corporation, by reassuring small depositors, merely served to relieve them from the necessity for keeping a watchful eye on the bankers. The banking system remained free to follow the same policies which had contributed to the depression.

The New Deal's programs for industry and for agriculture were no more fundamental. The NRA was hailed as a measure for restoring buying power and increasing employment. The act provided that "codes of fair competition" be drafted for each trade or industrial association, and suspended the anti-trust laws for the industries complying with the codes. This was exactly what Big Business had been demanding: it was the program the United States Chamber of Commerce had endorsed.

Promptly the leaders of each industry, buttressed by legal advisers who were experts in evading the anti-trust laws, assembled and wrote the existing trade-association agreements into the codes. They fixed prices, and gave the sanction of law to monopolistic practices.

In effect, the total operation of the NRA created a corporate state apparatus in which the full control of the industrial system was vested in the hands of Big Business. It was not different, in essence, from the corporate state created by Mussolini in Fascist Italy. As liberals perceived this effect, they began to denounce the act. Senator Borah declared the whole purpose of the system had been to fix prices and perpetuate monopoly. It had, they contended, retarded recovery, embittered labor relations, and failed to provide employment. Clarence Darrow subjected the NRA to caustic analysis and pronounced it "a regimented organization for exploitation."

The Agricultural Adjustment Act was an equally futile and ill-advised effort to apply scarcity economics and price fixing to a depressed segment of the economy. Under the Act, the AAA made benefit payments for crop reduction and for "plowing under the little pigs"—at a time when 15,000,000 families were living on public and private charity. It raised cotton prices—by almost exactly the amount the dollar had been devalued—and it added almost a million people to the relief rolls from the cotton area. It proved, in short, to be no solution for the social and economic needs of the underprivileged farmer.

In all of this, as Frances Perkins points out in *The Roosevelt I Knew,* the President himself had no coherent and consistent program. Roosevelt played by ear—the ear of the politician which was always close to the ground.

Moreover, some of the more worthwhile items in the New Deal program like the Wagner Act (and the REA)—

which liberals could view with pride and support with satisfaction—met the President's opposition when they were first presented. Their enactment was due to the insistence of such progressives as Robert Wagner, Hugo Black, Bob LaFollette, Burton Wheeler, and others who were not completely in the Democratic entourage. Whatever blessing they received from the Administration came only after they had proved to be politically profitable.

The record of these programs and panaceas, even with the addition of some basic pieces of social legislation which the progressives brought, does not add up to a coherent social or economic philosophy. Instead, the economic experiments, the expedients, the promises, and the constant avowals of high purposes were primarily for the political purpose of keeping the voters at the polls. The relief rolls, the WPA, and the PWA became integral parts of the system, and it was not until the war came that unemployment ended and the plants could work to capacity.

Yet when the war ended, the few New Dealers left in the Government had still no intelligible blueprint for producing the 60 million jobs they had so glibly promised. Since there had never been a single, basic philosophy in the New Deal, the death of Roosevelt and the emergence of Trumanism left the New Dealers without even a great man to follow. Some of the liberals, seeking order amid chaos, drifted into an active or passive endorsement of Stalinism. Others had no remedy except a permanent war economy, a peacetime draft, a more vigorous imperialism, and a war with Russia. The New Deal was dead because it had attempted to solve economic and social ills with political pills. It was dead—and with it had died much of the idealism its supporters had once proclaimed.

# CHAPTER ELEVEN

# THE WALLACE MOVEMENT

In the last days of 1947—in that week between Christmas and New Years which, in journalistic tradition, is notoriously weak in "news value"—Henry Agard Wallace announced his independent candidacy for the presidency of the United States. In so doing, Wallace took his stand in history with a long and impressive list of leaders of political revolt against the American two-party system—with such men as William Wirt, Theodore Roosevelt, Ben Butler, Peter Cooper, Millard Fillmore, General James B. Weaver, Horace Greeley, and "Fighting Bob" LaFollette.

Wallace's announcement, promptly seized upon by editors and radio commentators in what would otherwise have been a dull week, restored—or appeared to restore—to the American scene a "third party" to combat the political monopoly of the Democrats and the Republicans.

Significantly, the present national legislature is the first Congress in many years and one of the few in American political history in which no member wears the forlorn label of a minor party. While it is true that some Senators and Congressmen—notably the Kremlin-minded and Wallace-supported Vito Marcantonio of New York—had been candidates of a minor party as well as of a major one, all had taken their seats with either the Democrats or the Republicans. The Progressives, the Farmer-Laborites, the Unionists, the Populists, Greenbackers, Know-Nothings, Free-

Soilers, Anti-Masons, and Quids—the list is long and relatively honorable—of former days have no successors in the national capitol of 1948.

For many months before December 29, 1947, Wallace's candidacy had been incubating. For more than a year after President Truman unceremoniously ousted him from the cabinet, Wallace had been attacking, with increasing sharpness, the Truman Administration, the Truman Doctrine, and Marshall's policies.

In January, 1947, the Progressive Citizens of America, formed by a consolidation of the National Citizens Political Action Committee and the Independent Citizens Committee of the Arts, Sciences, and Professions—both dominated by Fellow-Travellers of the Communists—adopted Wallace as their spokesman. Throughout the year, to the intense disgust of the Americans for Democratic Action—an anti-Communist group sponsored by such old New Dealers as Mrs. Eleanor Roosevelt, Leon Henderson, and Chester Bowles—the PAC promoted Wallace meetings marked by well-paid attendance, superb stage-management, and well-organized claques. At these meetings, in speeches during the spring in England and France, and in his *New Republic* editorials, Wallace elaborated, with many a bumbling inconsistency, his opposition to President Truman and all his works. Yet some political observers found it difficult to believe that Wallace, who had loyally supported Roosevelt after FDR had discarded him, would ever leave the Democratic Party. But when, a few weeks before he announced his own candidacy, the self-proclaimed heir of Roosevelt's mantle declared he would prefer Taft to Truman, even the unbelieving realized that Wallace was preparing the way for a new—if somewhat peculiar—third party.

Henry Wallace brought to his candidacy a long connection with the New Deal which gave substance to his claim to be one of the most loyal of Roosevelt's adherents. A review of his record in this connection will serve to throw some interesting light on his possibilities as a third party candidate for the presidency.

As Secretary of Agriculture in Roosevelt's first administration, Wallace administered, it will be recalled, the unique AAA program—"plowing under the little pigs" they said of it—for the benefit of the large farmers and to the distress of share-croppers and tenants. So effectively did he follow the shifting policies of his chief—characteristically appearing as the saintly, high-minded apologist for each new expedient of the New Deal—that in 1940 Roosevelt, determining on a third term for himself, dictated Wallace's choice as vice-president.

Down to the time of his inauguration as vice-president, Wallace had been identified with the middle-western isolationists. In his book, *The American Choice,* published in 1940, he proposed to leave Europe—and the rest of the world—to Germany while the United States built up its security in the western hemisphere. But as vice-president, Wallace abandoned isolationism and gladly kept pace with each of the "steps short of war." With the coming of the war, Wallace assumed the role of prophet and became the chief spokesman of America's idealistic war aims. As Roosevelt lost interest in an earlier-professed idealism and became more of a "realist" in the game of world power politics, and more of a practical military strategist, Wallace assumed the function of heralding the coming "Century of the Common Man."

In addition to elaborating the concept that "this is a

fight between a free world and a slave world" and that "the century that will come out of this war can and must be the century of the common man," Wallace served as chairman of the potent Board of Economic Warfare, whose major purpose was the finding and promotion of war materials in other countries. In the course of his responsibilities in this connection, Wallace attempted, with little success, to raise the wages of tin miners in Bolivia and to promote liberal regimes in Latin American countries. His efforts met criticism both at home and abroad, and in the middle of 1943 his long smoldering fight with Jesse Jones, conservative Secretary of Commerce and head of the Federal Loan Agency, came into the open. Angered by the public recriminations between the two, Roosevelt discharged Wallace from his post and delivered the Board of Economic Warfare to one of Jones' men. Despite this treatment, Wallace remained loyal and continued to proclaim Roosevelt as the leader of the common man

In the following spring, Roosevelt sent Wallace on a "goodwill" tour to China and Siberia. There Wallace praised the "mature wisdom" of Chiang Kai-Shek and found the forced-labor deportees of the Soviet in Siberia to be comparable to the pioneers of the American frontier! Upon his return to the busy environs of the Potomac, he discovered, to his dismay, that Roosevelt did not want him again for vice-president. However, the travelling prophet refused to give up, wormed a weasel-worded endorsement from the President, and entered the lists of the Democratic convention in Chicago. But Roosevelt had endorsed other aspirants, and a combination of city machines and Southern conservatives brought the nomination—and eventually the presidency—to Harry Truman. Yet, to the amazement of everyone—except possibly Roosevelt—Henry campaigned vigorously for a fourth term for the man who had discarded him.

This loyalty, exceeding that of any other of Roosevelt's supporters, was duly rewarded.  At the beginning of the fourth term, the President offered his erstwhile vice-president any cabinet post except that of Secretary of State. Wallace promptly chose the Department of Commerce, and Roosevelt obligingly asked Jesse Jones to vacate his post at the head of that agency, pointing out that Wallace, who "gave of his utmost toward the victory," wanted the place. Just as obligingly, Jones resigned, but Congress promptly took the important Federal Loan Agency out of his bailiwick and Wallace assumed control of a forlorn Commerce Department.

There he remained: past the death of Roosevelt, the accession of Truman, the resignation of Ickes—even past his pro-Russian Madison Square Garden speech—until at last, at the insistence of Secretary of State Byrnes, Truman asked him to leave.  But his unemployment was of short duration. Much to his good fortune, publisher Michael Straight lost no time in offering him the job of chief copy reader on the *New Republic*.

Throughout his years as vice-president, as Secretary of Commerce, and as editor of the *New Republic*, Wallace's utterances increasingly identified him with the Communist line.  In the course of the late war, he proclaimed that Russia was an "economic democracy" while the United States was a "political" one.  At the close of the war, he proposed dividing the world between the Russians and the Americans—essentially a return to the isolationist, hemispheric-security dogma he had enunciated in *The American Choice* in 1940.  In a controversy with Bernard Baruch on atomic control, he proposed, in his capacity as Secretary of Commerce, that the United States give Russia the atomic bomb—more or less. In the spring of 1947, speaking as a peripatetic editor, he advised England about Russia's virtues and condemned as "imperialistic" the Truman Doctrine. In the months that followed, Wallace found much to condemn in the American policy and only praise for Russia. He insisted, however, that he remained a loyal devotee of capitalistic free enterprise.

\*   \*   \*

Wallace's announcement of his presidential candidacy on a program of "peace and prosperity" brought a rash of speculations and a wholesale desertion of his sinking ship. The speculations concerned themselves, first of all, with the question whether Wallace could pull enough votes from the Democrats to insure a Republican victory in November, and whether that favored Taft's or Dewey's chances in getting the Republican nomination. Democratic leaders insisted upon discounting Wallace's drawing power and even asserted that their party would be stronger without him. Republicans affected to be smug in the belief that Wallace only damaged their opponents.

A second line of speculation dealt with the problem whether Wallace himself would stay in the race for the presidency. Back in the summer of 1945 he had warned progressives against forming a national third party on the ground that it would only split the liberals and "guarantee a reactionary victory." In the meantime, of course, the Communist line had changed and, under "Comiform" inspiration, the Stalinists proposed forming third parties— chiefly as a means of stimulating a reaction from which they might profit. But it is significant that, at the very time that Wallace announced his independent candidacy, he cautiously pointed out that he would withdraw "should either of the major parties become definitely a peace party before the election." In view of this and his past performances in reversing his position, it is by no means certain that he will remain with the third party movement he has started.

It is a matter of small wonder, then, that the liberal-labor forces which Wallace hoped to lead don't want to have anything to do with him. The CIO unions, except those under Communist domination, are emphatically opposed to his candidacy. A. F. of L. unions—leaders and members—have also denounced his third party move vigorously.

Wallace has said that he expects support from Methodists and Quakers, but Methodists have never been pacifists and the Friends don't care for his wartime record. True, the Communists are all for him—which is all right with Wallace since "they are for peace"—but the rest of the left-wing wants no part of him. The *New Leader* has denounced him bitterly because of his Stalinism. Marshall Field's PM has taken the position that the "conditions for a meaningful third party" do not exist and that Wallace's third party campaign is "an adventurous move" likely to cause considerable damage.

Except for the *Daily Worker,* the Stalinist PCA, and the Communist-dominated rump of the once potent American Labor Party, Wallace's third party cannot count on any organized support.

\* \* \*

However, Henry Wallace's third party and the immediate response to his plea for liberals to "stand up and be counted" serves to bring into focus the political plight of the liberal and progressive forces of America. Wallace, who is half-right more often than he is right, devoted much of his initial "announcement" speech to condemning the policies of both the Democrats and the Republicans.

But there is nothing new in this. Long before Wallace, American liberals became distressed by the fact that the major political parties do not represent two well-defined lines of thought, two coherent and antipodal philosophies, and two clashing programs of action. Instead, among Republicans and Democrats alike there are Bourbon reactionaries and left-wingers, progressives and conservatives, pie-counter corruptionists and high-minded idealists. Long before Wallace, liberals began to nurse hopes of extracting their own kind from the old alignments and organizing them into a new political movement.

Wallace's party—whether it is a fixed star which will remain in the heavens through November, 1948, and even until 1952, or whether it is only a flash in the pan on the darkened horizon—at least serves to emphasize the problems and pitfalls which confront those who would realize the liberal dream.

# CHAPTER TWELVE

# OVERVIEW

The persistent phenomena of liberals and conservatives in each of the major parties—a phenomenon which has been deplored by progressives and denounced by Wallace—is chiefly the result of the variegated nature of American geography.

The rock-bound coast of Maine and the rain-soaked shores of California have different problems. Their social structure is differently formed. their economic life is differently oriented, and their cultures have different roots. So too are there differences between the cotton-belt and the dairyland, between the Appalachian hills and the arid areas of the West, between the wheatlands and the mill zones. Yet all the differences between the regions of America, and between groups within the region, have managed to find expression in two political organizations.

The strange nature of the American two-party system might perhaps be clarified by a glance at a situation which goes to the opposite extreme. Holland is a small country whose 12,000 square miles could be dropped from sight in any corner of the United States. Its pre-war population was less than nine millions. Yet more than 40 political parties contest Dutch elections, and proportional representation insures that a substantial number of them have seats in the States-General.

Normally the Catholics win the larger number, but the Social Democrats, the Anti-Revolutionists, the Christian

Historicals, the National Socialists, the Liberty Unionists, and the Communists have considerable delegations while a score of lesser parties, with one or two seats each, sometimes can make life miserable for the dominant groups. Seldom does any party control a majority of the seats in the legislature.

After an election in Holland the Queen calls upon the leader of a major party to "form a government." The putative prime minister then attempts to gather support from the other parties—promising a cabinet post to a leader of one group, pledging support for the special legislative pets of another, granting patronage favors to a third.

If these methods succeed in winning support of a majority of the States-General, he reports to the monarch, is named premier, and proceeds to organize the government. He has, in effect, formulated a political platform by compromising sundry divergent interests. So long as he can hold his groups together, his government exists. When one group breaks the majority combination, the Queen seeks another premier or appeals to the electorate in another election.

The formal processes of Dutch politics stand in startling contrast to American political practices. Yet, in essence the American and the Dutch varieties of political "democracy" have much in common. A Hollander looking at the American scene might fairly conclude that the United States has as many parties, in the Dutch sense, as his own Netherlands.

Each of the regional groups, each personal following, each peculiar bias or partial program which would produce a separate party in Holland is merged into either the Democratic or the Republican political conglomeration in the United States. In America these groups make their compromises and their combinations *before,* rather than after,

the election, and they present two allegedly alternate programs to the electorate.

In reality, an American "government" is no more cohesive
nor coherent than a Dutch government. Normally—unless
he can evade the necessity by some trumped-up "emergency"
—a President must select his cabinet from among the divergent factions of his "party." Normally, the acts and the
legislation of an administration are as much the result of
compromise between factional groups as the acts of a Dutch
"government." Normally, too, the platforms of the major
political combinations are necessarily vague, insipid, and
vacuous. The basic problem of Presidents in the United
States is the same as that of prime ministers in Holland:
keeping the factions balanced by a judicious juggling of
patronage and by a wise adjustment of legislative programs.

Throughout American history, the necessary compromises
between ideological, regional, and personal factions has
made each of the major parties conservative, and has made
them much alike. Repeatedly, a "liberal" party has come
to life in the United States, or an old party has been "liberal-
ized," only to fall into compromises and drift into conservatism. Thomas Jefferson's Republicans, ancestors of the
present Democrats, swept into office in 1800 with a liberal
dogma on their lips and a liberal program to enact. Twenty
years later the sands had run out, and the party's President
was the timid, time-serving, and insipidly conservative James
Monroe.

In 1828, Andrew Jackson, roaring "Let the people rule,"
began the curious "Jacksonian Democracy." Two decades
later his emasculated party was led by conservative medio-
crities Lewis Cass, Franklin Pierce, and James Buchanan.

In 1860 the Republicans, mouthing high humanitarianism and fervid patriotism, put Abraham Lincoln in the White House. Twenty years later they were safely in bed with big business. It took about the same time for the Democrats to move from Bryan to Cox, and the Republicans to go from Teddy Roosevelt to Harding—and even less time for the New Deal to produce Harry Truman.

Because the two major parties have regularly tended towards mediocrity and conservatism, discordant groups have frequently attempted to erect third parties to challenge the two major parties. John Randolph's Quids were only a splinter from Jefferson's Republicans, but the Anti-Masons, the Workers Parties of 1828, the Know-Nothings, Free-Soilers, Greenbackers, Populists, and Progressives were major efforts to inject third parties into the political arena. Often these third parties sent members to Congress, sometimes they influenced legislation, and occasionally they even educated the electorate. But each effort failed in its basic objective to capture power and the members eventually formed merely a faction of one or the other of the major political combinations.

# CHAPTER THIRTEEN

# THE OBSTACLES AHEAD

Liberals and progressives, farmers and lib-labs, well-meaning idealists and political sore-heads who dream of a permanent liberal party in the United States usually wind up by being appalled at the obstacles which confront them. Each time a new group assembles to scan the political skies, the clouds of doubt and timidity obscure their vision— and always present in such gathering are those who hold out the lure that somehow, some way the liberals can capture the party of Pepper and Hague, Truman and Kelly, or else the party of Morse and Taft, Bricker and Stassen, and Hoover and Dewey.

If the history of liberal movements in American politics points anywhere, it indicates the futility of liberals following the downward pathway of fusion, confusion, and diffusion. Time after time liberals have entered the old parties, only to find themselves placated with palliatives and their program perverted to partisanship. At best they have obtained some reforms, but never has a complete liberal program found its way into the laws of the land. In the end the liberals have invariably been betrayed. Experience should indicate that the progressive forces must travel the hard way to their goal. The short-cuts are strewn with booby-traps.

But the obstacles that line the hard way are indeed discouraging. In general, they fall into two classes, the practical and the philosophical, and neither can be dismissed as unimportant. Both are imperatives—liberals must find a base upon which to make a valid appeal to the reason and conscience of the voters, and they must create a practical organization to carry out the program.

The practical handicaps which a new liberal party must overcome fall into two groups: financial and legal. These are the obstacles which scare the timid and discourage the indolent. These two are the ones to which the proponents of fusion always point — even though they forget to mention that the same problems would face liberals in an attempt to win one of the old parties. Nevertheless, candor compels the admission that the barriers are formidable indeed.

The financial obstacles can be easily stated. A permanent liberal party must have money to compete with the old parties. The amount needed is enormous, for a new liberal party would have to combat the concentrated wealth of the manufacturers and the bankers, of the railroad companies and the airlines. It would have to fight, as well, against the power of the United States Treasury, the entrenched bureaucracy, and the contractors who profit from Government spending. A new liberal party would need money for radio programs, for campaigning with special trains, automobiles, and airplanes. It would need money for campaign literature and newspaper advertising. And it would need more money than either of the old parties, for it would have none of the advantages of earlier publicity—the continuing returns of money already spent.

Such money could not come from individual contributors. Socialists for years have tried to support a party on membership dues and plaintive appeals for pittances. The Non-Partisan League tried membership dues and met failure.

Nor could money come to a liberal party from the time-honored practice of blackmail—frying the fat cats who have grown sleek on governmental largesse. In the early days the Bolsheviki financed their organization by robbing banks, but a new liberal party would probably refrain from such fund-raising methods.

Some money, of course, could be raised by memberships, and a great deal could come in the collection plates of a truly evangelical liberalism. Some, too, might come from co-operatives—and will as soon as taxpayers' alliances and the NAM succeed in driving the co-ops from their non-partisan position. But the only available source of large amounts for a liberal program is in the labor unions, some of whom (though by no means all) might endorse and support a progressive political party.

Although the financial handicaps for a new liberal party may be exaggerated and may be overcome, the legal obstacles in the way of a third party furnish additional hurdles. In many states, the two old parties are as firmly entrenched in the laws as the Communist Party in Russia. White primaries and poll-tax provisions in some Southern states are notorious. More serious though less publicized, are the procedural controls in other states by which new parties and independent candidates are handicapped. It is, in fact, easier for a new party to get its candidates on the ballot in some of the poll-tax states than in most of the states where universal suffrage prevails.

The situation is roughly as follows:

In Alabama, a state convention may make nominations and any group can hold a convention.

In Arizona, 3,000 signatures can place a party slate on the ballot.

In Arkansas candidates need from 50 to 1,000 signatures, depending on the locality, to get on the "independent" column.

More difficult is California. Its 22 electoral votes are protected by a requirement that a new party petition have the signatures of 10% of all voters—over 200,000 names—10 months before the election.

In Colorado, 500 signatures are required, but they must be individually notarized.

Connecticut requires 8,000 signatures.

In little Delaware a third party needs 500 signatures in each of the state's three counties.

Florida and Georgia require the signatures of 5% of the voters in the previous election.

In Idaho a convention of 200 people on the second Tuesday of June can nominate a ticket.

Illinois presents a more difficult situation. There, 25,000 signatures are needed and they must include 200 from each of 50 counties.

Indiana requires ½ of 1% of the voters at the last general election—roughly from 8,000 to 10,000 names.

Iowa requires only a convention.

Kansas will admit candidates to the independent column with only a handful of signatures.

One thousand signers are needed in Kentucky, but 15,000 are required in Louisiana.

The 1,000 signatures needed in Maine must be individually notarized.

Maryland requires 2,000 signatures.

In Massachusetts a complicated system of district conventions provide a considerable set of obstacles.

Under Michigan law nominating petitions, with 6,500 signers, must be filed six months before the election.

Minnesota's law prohibits collecting signatures before primary day—which is only 30 days from the filing date—but requires only 2,000.

Mississippi's candidates must be backed by 50 to 1,000 signatures.

Missouri probably requires an act of the legislature.

Montana requires only a convention.

In Nebraska, a convention of 750 electors who would sign an agreement to form a new party would suffice.

Nevada's new party would need signatures from 5% of the voters.

New Hampshire wants 1,000 notarized signatures.

New Mexico requires a convention.

New York wants 12,000 signatures, including at least 50 in each county of the state.

North Carolina demands 10,000 signatures, and those signing must join the party or be prosecuted for fraud.

North Dakota admits candidates to the independent column on the same basis as those in the regular columns.

Oregon requires a convention of 250.

Ohio needs 10% of the voters in the last gubernatorial election—200,000 names.

In Oklahoma 5,000 signatures are necessary.

In Pennsylvania 10,000 signatures must be filed in April preceding the election.

Rhode Island's 500 must be notarized.

South Carolina is easy. Any party can hold its own primaries and print and distribute its own ballots.

South Dakota wants 6,000 signatures.

Tennessee, Texas, Virginia, Washington, and Wyom. require state conventions.

In Vermont and West Virginia 1% of the vote is necessary.

Utah requires 500 signatures.

Wisconsin candidates must have the backing of 5% of the voters.

In actual fact, these legal obstacles are more apparent than real. Except in a few states, a new party with a mass following would have relatively little trouble in getting its candidates on the ballot. In a dozen states, with 106 electoral votes, simple party conventions can launch a new party. In 10 others, with 64 votes, less than a thousand signatures are needed. On the other hand, six states— California, Illinois, Louisiana, New York, New Jersey, and Ohio—with 150 electoral votes, need from 13,000 to 200,000 petitioners to get candidates into an independent column.

The implication of these figures is clear. A new political party must rest upon a broad popular foundation. With mass support neither the financial nor the legal obstacles need prove insuperable. The practical work of organization cannot be neglected, but the major task before liberals and progressives is agreement upon principles. Only after that agreement can the labor of organization begin.

# CHAPTER FOURTEEN

# THE OPPORTUNITIES AHEAD

A permanent liberal party must face many obstacles in achieving realization of its goals. Those which have been most publicized—the difficulties of getting on the ballot and of financing a new party—are the least important. If a new party has a sufficiently broad popular base, and enough willing workers to contribute time and money to the cause, the technical obstacles embodied in the electoral laws of the several states can be readily overcome.

Far more important is the difficulty in finding a popular base, in formulating a program and a policy which will unite farmers and laborers in a single party. Historically the representatives of the agrarian and the liberal-labor traditions have been at opposite poles of political thought, and programs which could enlist the support of the one found the other passive or positively antagonistic. For the most part, the programs of the American Labor Party have received little attention in the agricultural sections even of New York, while the Non-Partisan Leagues, Progressive parties, and Farmer-Labor organizations of the Western areas have met scorn or indifference at the gates of the metropolitan districts. The urban workers have never rallied around the idea of the co-operatives, while farmers have been regularly suspicious of labor unions.

The American experience has demonstrated that the union of agrarians and lib-labs can be accomplished on a temporary basis and on a rhetorical program. Jefferson

united Western farmers and Aaron Burr's urban
in a campaign against the Federalist aristocracy.
brought the farmers into an alliance with Martin
Buren's loco-foco democracy. The New Deal, with rhetoric,
slogans, and a catch-as-catch-can program, taking advantage
of times of stress, rallied all "forgotten men" against the
"money changers in the temple." In other words, unity
of farmers and laborers can be accomplished by dramatic
personalities, by propaganda techniques, and for negative
ends, especially in times of emergency.

Yet despite the evidence from American political history of the difficulties in the way of organizing a liberal
party, the record contains both suggestions and promise for
a successful and permanent progressive party. There is,
for example, a solid core of liberal doctrine which is common to both the agrarian and the lib-lab traditions. There
is, in addition, a body of experience which offers both
warning and suggestion. There is no reason why the dreams
of the liberals cannot be realized, and a program of action
formulated which will unite, in a lasting alliance, the farmers and the workers of America.

The basic core of American liberal dogma—of which
many self-proclaimed liberals need to be reminded—contains at least four concepts which must lie at the foundation
of any progressive program. All four are deeply rooted
in the American heritage, and the alleged liberal who re-
jects any one of them is faithless to the progressive cause
he purports to represent.

First of the basic concepts of American liberalism is a
deep-seated opposition to doctrines of the police state. The
concept that government always knows better than the
people, that the bureaucracy is possessed of a superior wis-

dom, is foreign to the traditions of both the agrarians and the lib-labs. In its application this principle involves an opposition to militarism, to the increase of the standing army, and unalterable opposition to conscription.

It involves, too, drawing a sharp and rigid line between the service function of government, with its administrative machinery, and the assertion of governmental authority over areas of human life which can and must be regulated by voluntary co-operation. Government exists among men, according to the Declaration of Independence, to secure the rights of life, liberty, and the pursuit of happiness. But Jefferson, who wrote those words, knew that long exercise of power was destructive of freedom, and that eternal vigilance was the price of liberty.

Not long after he had written the Declaration of Independence, Jefferson wrote his *Notes on Virginia* in which he carefully defined the danger inherent in excessive governmental power. Seventy tyrants, he declared as he pointed to the Virginia legislature, might be as dangerous as one. From Jefferson to the present day, true liberals have maintained this vigilance and have eschewed all programs which threatened to increase the areas of governmental interference into affairs of men which could be regulated by voluntary co-operation.

Closely connected with this opposition to the police state is the progressive tradition of devotion to democracy and to democratic procedures. From the beginning of the American Government, liberals have experimented with new devices to make democracy work. The Jeffersonians made nugatory the Constitution's carefully rigged Electoral College; the Jacksonians warred upon the caucus system of nominations and adopted the nominating convention, while the Populists and Progressives promoted direct primaries for convention delegates.

The Jeffersonians and Jacksonians fought for universal white manhood suffrage, the Republicans extended the vote to Negroes, Populist-Progressive tradition produced woman suffrage, and latter-day liberals wage a winning battle against the poll-tax.

Down to World War I the liberal tradition produced new experiments in democracy, and it is high time that liberals turn their thoughts once more to devising democratic procedures for new areas of life. Labor unions might well experiment with democracy. In production and in distribution, the extension of co-operatives—probably with some modifications of doctrinaire Rochdale principles—might produce a more democratic control of economic institutions.

The third area in which all progressives—be they agrarians or lib-labs—can agree is in the injection of a sense of public responsibility into co-operatives, labor unions, and aggregations of capital. For too long progressives have blindly assumed that because labor unions benefited a large class of the population—and a class that was generally exploited—that unions were exempt from liberal criticism. Co-operatives, too, are "a good thing," but co-operatives whose offices are filled by nepotism and whose management is bureaucratic and conservative may be as lacking in a sense of public responsibility as a labor union which strikes against the general welfare or a business combination in restraint of trade which rigs prices. A truly liberal party will maintain the same vigilance on all institutions—remembering that one good system, losing a sense of public responsibility, might corrupt the world.

In addition, progressives of all traditions can unite in a rigid insistence on complete civil liberty for every shade of opinion and for all shades of skin. From the Bill of Rights to the last fight to release conscientious objectors from prison liberals have contended for men's rights to freedom of speech, of opinion, of assembly, and of worship.

These four—opposition to the police state, devotion to democratic processes, insistence upon complete social responsibility, and civil liberty—are the basic ingredients of any genuine liberal program. Upon these items liberals of all traditions can unite. Together they spell Reform—which is the first of the three R's of a new party.

The other two R's of a liberal party are Research and Regionalism—both suggested by the history of new party movements in the American past. The first of these, Research, implies planning, but it means more than the mere effort to implement a preconceived ideology. Socialists, and many other doctrinaires, have talked much of a "planned society," but, for the most part, their "plans" have consisted in rhetorical advocacy of theoretical blueprints for a better world.

More than "plans," the people of America need a scholarly and scientific examination of the facts of society, and a careful search for the best democratic method of social improvement. This implies sociological, economic, and political research, conducted by competent sociologists, economists, political scientists, and historians which might produce on a nation-wide scale that wedding of soil and seminar which once made Wisconsin a great progressive state.

Such research must not be a Government monopoly. Private and public planning must go hand in hand, while individuals and institutions, chambers of commerce and trade unions, co-operatives and industries must alike study the needs of society. From such studies—and only from such studies—can "plans" be made which will contribute to the fullest measure of human happiness. The reports which came from Herbert Hoover's commissions furnished the solid basis for most of the lasting contributions of the New Deal. A continuation of such studies might furnish the elements of permanence to any new liberal party.

Finally, it might be well for liberals and progressives to remember the basic regionalism of American life and of American politics. The United States has never been a closely integrated whole. Its resources are varied, its institutions spring from many sources, its geography is diverse, and its traditions are mixed. No successful political party has ever had a single coherent program for the entire country. Each party—Federalists, Jeffersonians, Whigs, Jacksonians, Democrats, and Republicans—has been a composite of regional groups held together by bargaining, conciliation, and compromise. Today, despite the increasing tendencies to centralization, the problems of the various regions remain different. In truth, a large part of the nation's problems spring from the attempts of dominant groups in some regions to impose their particular programs upon the entire country. A truly liberal program would proclaim the necessity of preserving the integrity of each separate region.

Regional planning, based upon solid research, might provide for the democratic development of each region's human and physical resources. On a program of regional development the liberals of each area of the country could unite in a harmonious and lasting party. Lib-labs and agrarians, Liberal Republicans and the progressive remnants of the Democrats, Progressives from the Middle West and liberals of the urban East could overcome the philosophical obstacles to a new party by recognizing that American problems differ from region to region and that one region's meat may be another region's poison.

Henry Wallace's third party movement isn't going anywhere. It can't. It has no genuine program. It is merely seeking to capitalize upon the opposition to both Trumanism and Taftism and upon a wholesome opposition to any more wars. This movement is tinged with Communism and is merely negative in its philosophy. Neither Wallace nor the Communists are opposed to unbridled bureaucracy, to a police state, nor to militarism. They oppose Truman's bureaucracy and Truman's anti-Russian militarism, but they only offer to substitute a new bureaucracy and a new police for the old.

Wallace and his Fellow Travelers are attempting once more to marshall the discontented and cement them with rhetoric until after the election. In an emergency—in depression or in case of a new war—their program may have momentary success. But without a coherent program of reform, without sound research into basic social and economic problems, and without due consideration for regional differences, the Wallace party offers liberals only an opportunity to cast a protest vote. A new liberal party must be based on something more solid than oratory, on something more positive than mere opposition.

Far sounder than Wallace's pro-Russian soreheadism is the movement for education for a new party headed by A. Philip Randolph. After two preliminary meetings of diverse liberal factions held in the winter of 1946-47, the group—with more caution than is usual in such gatherings

—formed a Committee on Education for a New Party. Two reports from this Committee show appreciation of regional differences and the need for careful study of social and economic problems. The tentative program shows a keen awareness of the need for democratic planning along TVA lines—planning which recognizes the need for over-all goals but emphasizes the urgent need for individual freedom and regional and local participation. This is sane, cautious liberalism—and an indication that the liberal and progressive forces of America can work together to build a new and better nation. On such a basis a genuine new party can be built.

The history of new party movements in the United States is filled with both warnings and suggestions, but it does not add up to a counsel of despair. The failures of the past can be avoided, and with a program of Reform, Research, and Regionalism—with opposition to totalitarianism in all its forms and a devotion to democratic processes—a new and lasting liberal party can yet emerge for the salvation of the nation.

# BIBLIOGRAPHY

## SPECIAL WORKS

*Third Party Movements Since the Civil War.* By F. E. Haynes, 1916.

*Labor and Farmer Parties in the U. S., 1828-1928.* By Nathan Fine, 1928.

*Farmers and Workers in American Politics.* By Stuart A. Rice, 1924.

*Toward a Farmer-Labor Party.* By Harry W. Laidler, 1938.

*The Coming of a New Party.* By Paul H. Douglas, 1932.

"Labor and Farmer Groups and the Three Party System." By J. R. Starr, *Southwestern Social Science Quarterly,* June, 1936.

"The Third Party Tradition in American Politics." By John D. Hicks, *Mississippi Valley Historical Review,* June, 1933.

*American Progressivism.* By Alfred J. Aagis, 1947.

*Social Politics in the United States.* By F. E. Haynes, 1924.

*National Party Platforms.* By K. H. Porter, 1924.

*Political Parties in the United States.* By James H. Hopkins, 1900.

*National Conventions and Platforms.* By Thomas H. McKee, 1900.

*The American Party System.* By Charles E. Merriam and Harold Gosnell, rev. ed., 1940.

*History of American Political Thought.* Raymond A. Gettell, 1928.

*The Evolution of American Political Parties.* By E. E. Robinson, 1924.

*American Parties and Elections.* By E. M. Sait, rev. ed., 1939.

*The Political Parties of Today.* By A. N. Holcombe, 1924.

*American Politics.* By Peter Odegard and E. A. Helms, 1938.

*Presidential Elections.* By C. A. M. Ewing, 1940.

*American Political Parties.* By W. E. Binkley, 1944.

## MISCELLANEOUS WORKS

*Confessions of a Reformer.* By Frederick C. Howe, 1925.

*They Also Ran: The Story of the Men Who Were Defeated for the Presidency.* By Irving Stone, 1943.

*Forty Years of It.* By Brand Whitlock, 1913.

*My Story.* By Tom Johnson, 1911.

*Farewell to Reform.* By John Chamberlain, 1932.

*Rebel America.* By Lillian Symes and Travers Clement, 1934.

*Crusaders for American Liberalism.* By Louis Filler, 1939.

*Liberalism in America.* By Harold E. Stearns, 1919.

*Art Young: His Life and Time.* By Art Young, 1939.

*Fighting Years.* By Oswald Garrison Villard, 1939.

*The Pursuit of Happiness.* By Herbert Agar, 1938.

*"Regions, Classes, and Sections in American History."* By William B. Hesseltine, *Journal of Land and Public Utility Economics,* Feb., 1944.
*Lost Men of American History.* By Stewart Holbrook, 1946.


## GENERAL WORKS

*Encyclopedia of the Social Sciences.* E. R. A. Seligman, Editor, 1930.
*The Encyclopedia of Social Reform.* Edited by William D. P. Bliss, 1897.
*The Growth of the American Republic.* By Samuel E. Morrison and Henry Commager, 1942.
*Rise of American Civilization.* By Charles and Mary Beard, 1930.
*The Significance of Sections in American History.* By F. J. Turner, 1932.
*The United States, 1830-1850.* By Frederick J. Turner, 1935.
*When the West is Gone.* By Frederick L. Paxon, 1930.
*The Politicos.* By Matthew Josephson, 1938.
*Only Yesterday.* By Frederick Lewis Allen, 1931.


## THE ROOTS OF REVOLT

*Third Party Movements Since the Civil War.* By F. E. Haynes, 1916.
*Labor and Farmer Parties in the U. S., 1828-1928.* By Nathan Fine, 1928.
*The Groundswell.* By Jonathan Periam, 1874.
*The Agrarian Crusade.* By Solon J. Buck, 1920.
*The Agrarian Movement in North Dakota.* By Paul Fossun, 1925.
*The Agrarian Revolution in Georgia.* By Robert P. Brooks, 1914.
*"Independent Parties in the West."* By Solon J. Buck in *Essays in American History Dedicated to Frederick J. Turner.*
*History of Political Parties in the State of New York.* By Jabez D. Hammond, 1842.
*History of the State of New York,* Vol. VI. By A. C. Flick, 1937. (Deals with the Working Man's Party.)
*The Barnburners.* By H. D. A. Donovan, 1926.


## AMERICAN (KNOW-NOTHING) PARTY

*Political Nativism in New York State.* By L. D. Scisco.
*History of the Know-Nothing Party in Maryland.* By L. F. Schmeckebier, 1897.
*Nativism in the Old Northwest, 1850-1860.* By M. E. Thomas.
*The Protestant Crusade, 1800-1860.* By Ray Allen Billington, 1938.
*"Know-Nothingism in Wisconsin."* By Joseph Schafer, *Wisconsin Magazine of History,* Vol. VII, 1924.
*The Know-Nothing Party.* By J. J. Desmond, 1905.

## ANTI-MASONIC PARTY

*The Anti-Masonic Party.* By Charles McCarthy, 1902.

*The Anti-Masonic Almanac for the Year 1833.* By Edward Giddens, 1933.

*Anti-Masonic Inquirer.* (A newspaper published by Thurlow Weed from 1826 to 1830.)

*Anti-Masonic Newspapers of New York.* By M. W. Hamilton, 1940.

## EQUAL RIGHTS PARTY (LOCOFOCOS)

*History of the Locofoco or Equal Rights Party.* By Fitzwilliam Byrdsall, 1842.

"Diverging Tendencies in New York Democracy in the Period of the Locofocos." By William Trimble, *American Historical Review,* June, 1919.

## FREE SOIL PARTY

*The Liberty and Free-Soil Parties in the Northwest.* By Theodore C. Smith, 1897.

*History of the People of the United States.* By J. B. McMaster, 1913.

## GRANGER MOVEMENT

*The Granger Movement.* By Solon J. Buck, 1913.

*History of the Granger Movement.* By E. W. Martin, 1874.

*The Granger Movement in Illinois.* By A. E. Paine, 1904.

## GREENBACK MOVEMENT

*A History of the Greenbacks.* By Wesley C. Mitchell, 1903.

*The Greenback Movement of 1875-1884 and Wisconsin's Part In It.* By E. B. Usher, 1911.

## POPULIST (PEOPLE'S) PARTY

*Biography of Ignatius Donnelly.* By E. W. Fish, 1892.

*Lives of Weaver and Fields, and Achievements of the People's Party.* By E. A. Allen, 1892.

*The Populist Revolt.* By John D. Hicks, 1939.

*The Populist Movement.* By F. L. McVey, 1896.

*The Populist Movement in the U. S.* By Anna Rochester, 1943.

*The Populist Movement in Georgia.* By Alex Arnett, 1922.

*The Tillman Movement in South Carolina.* By Francis B. Simkins, 1926.

## WHIG PARTY

*The Whig Party in the South.* By Arthur C. Cole, 1913.

*The Decline of Aristocracy in the Politics of New York.* By Dixon Ryan Fox, 1918.

## THE BULL MOOSE MOVEMENT AND THE
## PROGRESSIVES OF 1924

*The Progressive Movement.* By Benjamin P. DeWitt, 1915.

*The Progressive Movement of 1924.* By Kenneth C. McKay, 1947.

*Beveridge and the Progressive Era.* By Claude G. Bowers, 1932.

*Autobiography of William Allen White,* 1946.

*Wisconsin: An Experiment in Democracy.* By Frederick C. Howe, 1917.

*The Wisconsin Idea.* By Charles McCarthy, 1912.

"Who Killed the Progressive Party?" By Harold Ickes, *American Historical Review,* Jan., 1941.

*Breaking New Ground.* By Gifford Pinchot, 1947.

*Autobiography of a Curmudgeon.* By Harold Ickes, 1943.

*Myself.* By John R. Commons, 1934.

*Fighting Liberal.* By George W. Norris, 1945.

*The Progressive.* (Weekly from 1936 to 1947; Monthly, 1948).

*Insurgency: Personalities and Politics of the Taft Era.* By Kenneth W. Hechler, 1940.

### THE LAFOLLETTES

*LaFollette's Autobiography.* By Robert M. LaFollette, 1913.

*LaFollette's Winning of Wisconsin, 1894-1904.* By A. O. Barton, 1922.

*The LaFollettes and the Wisconsin Idea.* By Edward Doan, 1948.

### THEODORE ROOSEVELT

*Theodore Roosevelt and the Progressive Movement.* By George Mowry, 1946.

*Theodore Roosevelt.* By Henry F. Pringle, 1931.

*Progressive Principles.* By Theodore Roosevelt, 1913.

### THE SOCIALIST PARTY

*History of Socialism in the U. S.* By Morris Hillquit, 1910.

*A History of Socialist Thought.* By Harry W. Laidler, 1927.

*Debs: His Life, Writings, and Speeches.* By Eugene V. Debs, 1910.

*History of American Socialisms.* By J. H. Noyes, 1870.

*What Is Our Destiny?* By Norman Thomas, 1944.

### LABOR SATELLITE PARTIES

*Labor and Farmer Parties in the United States, 1828-1928.* By Nathan Fine, 1928.

*Labor and Politics.* By M. R. Carroll, 1923.

*Farmers and Workers in American Politics.* By Stuart A. Rice, 1924.

*History of Labor in the United States.* By John R. Commons and Associates, 1918.

*National Labor Federations in the U. S.* By William Kirk, 1906.

*American Labor.* By Herbert Harris, 1939.

*The Labor Movement in America.* By M. C. Clark and S. F. Simon, 1938.

*History of the Labor Movement in the U. S.* By Philip S. Foner, 1947.

*The Knights of St. Crispin.* By D. D. Lescohier, 1910.

"The Coming Labor Party." By Paul W. Ward, *The Nation,* April 15, 1936

## AMERICAN FEDERATION OF LABOR

*My Seventy Years of Life and Labor.* By Samuel Gompers, 1925.

*The American Federation of Labor.* By Lewis Lorwin, 1933.

*Labor and Democracy.* By William Green, 1939.

## CONGRESS OF INDUSTRIAL ORGANIZATIONS

*When Labor Organizes.* By Robert R. R. Brooks, 1937.

*The First Round: The Story of the CIO Political Action Committee.* Edited by Joseph Gaer, 1944.

## INDUSTRIAL WORKERS OF THE WORLD

*The I. W. W.: A Study of American Syndicalism.* By Paul F. Brissenden, 1919.

*Decline of the I. W. W.* By John Gambs, 1932.

## KNIGHTS OF LABOR

*History of Labor in the United States,* Vol. II. By John R. Commons and associates, 1918.

*The Labor Movement, 1868-1890.* By Norman Ware, 1929.

*Thirty Years of Labor, 1859-1889.* By Terence V. Powderly, 1889.

## THE AGRARIAN REVOLT

*The Agriculture Bloc.* By Arthur Capper, 1922.

*The Farm Bloc.* By Wesley McCune, 1943.

*The Agrarian Movement in North Dakota.* By Paul R. Fossun, 1925.

*The Farmer's Last Frontier.* By Fred A. Shannon, 1945.

## NONPARTISAN LEAGUE

*The Nonpartisan League.* By Herbert E. Gaston, 1920.

*The Nonpartisan League.* By Andrew Bruce, 1921.

*The Story of the Nonpartisan League.* By Charles E. Russell, 1920.

"The Expansion and Decline of the Nonpartisan League in the Western Middlewest." By Theodore Salutos, *Agricultural History*, Oct., 1946.

"The Rise of the Nonpartisan League in North Dakota." By Theodore Salutos, *Agricultural History*, Jan., 1946.

## THE REPUBLICAN PARTY — PAST AND PRESENT

*The Formation of the Republican Party.* By G. S. P. Kleeburg, 1911.

*The Republican Party . . . 1854-1904.* By Francis Curtis, 1904.

*The Republican Party: A History.* By William S. Myers, 1928.

*History of the Republican National Conventions.* By John Tweedy, 1910.

*Early History of the Republican Party.* By W. C. Crandall, 1930.

*The Liberal Republican Movement.* By E. D. Ross, 1919.

*Insurgency: Personalities and Politics of the Taft Era.* By Kenneth W. Hechler, 1940.

*Borah of Idaho.* By Claudius O. Johnson, 1936.

*The Hoover Policies.* By Ray Lyman Wilbur and Arthur Hyde, 1937.

*The Hoover Administration.* By W. S. Myers and W. H. Newton, 1936.

*Incredible Era: The Life and Times of Warren Harding.* By Samuel H. Adams, 1939.

*Autobiography of William Allen White*, 1946.

*William Howard Taft.* By Herbert S. Duffy, 1930.

*Beveridge and the Progressive Era.* By Claude G. Bowers, 1932.

*Where I Stand.* By Harold Stassen, 1947.

## THE NEW DEAL — PAST AND PRESENT

*The History of the New Deal, 1933-1938.* By Basil Rauch, 1944.

*After Seven Years.* By Raymond Moley, 1939.

*The New Dealers.* By "Unofficial Observor," 1934.

*The Blue Eagle: From Egg to Earth.* By Hugh Johnson, 1935.

*The 168 Days.* By Joseph Alsop and Turner Catledge, 1938.

*Jim Farley's Story.* By James A. Farley, 1948.

*Economic Consequences of the New Deal.* By Benjamin Stolberg and Warren Vinton, 1935.

*Depression Decade: From New Era Through New Deal, 1929-1941.* By Broadus Mitchell, 1947.

*They Voted for Roosevelt.* By E. E. Robinson, 1947.

*Confessions of a Congressman.* By Jerry Voorhis, 1947.

## FRANKLIN D. ROOSEVELT

*Mr. Roosevelt.* By Compton Mackenzie, 1944.

*The Roosevelt I Knew.* By Frances Perkins, 1946.

*Nothing to Fear: The Selected Addresses of Franklin D. Roosevelt.* Edited by B. D. Zevin, 1946.

*The Public Papers and Addresses of Franklin D. Roosevelt.* Compiled by Samuel Rosenman, 1938 and 1941.

"Roosevelt: A First Appraisal by Those Who Knew Him." *New Republic,* Special Supplement, April 15, 1946.

### HARRY TRUMAN

*Missouri Compromise.* By Tris Coffin, 1947.

*Harry Truman.* By William Helm, 1947.

*Truman Speaks.* Edited by Cyril Clemens, 1946.

*This Man Truman.* By Frank McNaughton and Walter Hehmeyer, 1945.

### WILLIAM JENNINGS BRYAN

*The Memoirs of William Jennings Bryan.* By William J. Bryan, 1925.

*The Peerless Leader.* By Paxton Hibben, 1929.

*The First Battle: A Story of the Campaign of 1896.* By William Jennings Bryan, 1896.

"Myths of the Bryan Campaign." By James A. Barnes, *Missouri Valley Historical Review,* Dec., 1947.

### ANDREW JACKSON

*The Age of Jackson.* By Arthur F. Schlesinger, Jr., 1945.

"Did Labor Support Andrew Jackson·" By William A. Sullivan, *Political Science Quarterly,* Dec., 1947.

### THE WALLACE MOVEMENT

*Henry Wallace: The Man and the Myth.* By Dwight Macdonald, 1948.

*An Uncommon Man: Or Henry Wallace and Sixty Million Jobs.* By Frank Kingdon, 1945.

*The Wallaces of Iowa.* By Russell Lord, 1947.

"Stand Up and Be Counted." By Henry A. Wallace, *New Republic,* January 5, 1948.

"Third Parties and the American Tradition." By Henry A. Wallace, *New Republic,* January 19, 1948.

"The New Republic and Third Parties." By Michael Straight, *New Republic,* January 19, 1948.

*New Frontiers.* By Henry A. Wallace, 1934.

*The American Choice.* By Henry A. Wallace, 1940.

*Whose Constitution?* By Henry A. Wallace, 1940.

## COMMUNIST PARTY

*American Communism.*  By James Oneal and G. A. Werner, 1947.

*I Confess: The Truth About American Communism.*  By Benjamin Gitlow, 1939.

*The Red Decade.*  By Eugene Lyons, 1941.

*This Is My Story.*  By Louis Budenz, 1947.

*Communism in the United States.*  By Earl Browder, 1935.

*What Is Communism?*  By Earl Browder, 1936.